Jack Qu

W9-BOI-387

The Art of Reading
Part I

Professor Timothy Spurgin

THE TEACHING COMPANY ®

PUBLISHED BY:

THE TEACHING COMPANY
4840 Westfields Boulevard, Suite 500
Chantilly, Virginia 20151-2299
1-800-TEACH-12
Fax—703-378-3819
www.teach12.com

Copyright © The Teaching Company, 2009

Printed in the United States of America

This book is in copyright. All rights reserved.

Without limiting the rights under copyright reserved above,
no part of this publication may be reproduced, stored in
or introduced into a retrieval system, or transmitted,
in any form, or by any means
(electronic, mechanical, photocopying, recording, or otherwise),
without the prior written permission of
The Teaching Company.

ISBN 1-59803-568-1

Credits begin on page 216 and constitute a continuation
of the copyright page.

Timothy Spurgin, Ph.D.

Bonnie Glidden Buchanan Professor of English Literature
Lawrence University

Dr. Timothy Spurgin grew up in Mankato, Minnesota. He graduated magna cum laude from Carleton College, where he wrote his senior thesis on the role of realism in the English and American novel. During his senior year, he was also elected to Phi Beta Kappa and chosen as the student commencement speaker. On the encouragement of his teachers at Carleton, he applied for and received a Mellon Fellowship in the Humanities. He went on to do his graduate work at the University of Virginia, earning an M.A. and a Ph.D. in English Literature. Dr. Spurgin's doctoral dissertation focused on the novels of Charles Dickens.

Since 1990, Dr. Spurgin has taught at Lawrence University in Appleton, Wisconsin. His teaching includes courses on romanticism and contemporary critical theory, as well as a course on the English novel. While at Lawrence, Dr. Spurgin has received two awards for teaching: the Outstanding Young Teacher Award and the Freshman Studies Teaching Prize. He has twice served as director of Lawrence's freshman program, recognized as one of the best in the nation, and has three times received the Babcock Award, voted on by Lawrence students for the person who "through involvement and interaction with students has made a positive impact on the campus community."

Dr. Spurgin's writing has appeared in *The Chronicle of Higher Education*, *Dickens Studies Annual*, and *Dickens Quarterly*. He previously published a course with The Teaching Company called *The English Novel*. He lives in Appleton with his wife, Gretchen Revie, and their wheaten terrier, Penny.

Table of Contents
The Art of Reading
Part I

©2009 The Teaching Company.

The Art of Reading

Scope:

We all know how to read, but how many of us know how to read well?

This course is designed to encourage the habit of artful reading. Its purpose is not so much to impart information as to sharpen skills and inspire confidence. By the end of the course, you should be ready to dive into almost any work of fiction—no matter who the author may be—since you will have gained a deeper understanding of how such works can be approached and enjoyed.

Throughout the course, we consider big ideas and juicy examples, ranging from the classic to the contemporary and back again. We not only look at Charles Dickens and Leo Tolstoy, but also stop to consider the works of Lorrie Moore and Jhumpa Lahiri. We also bring authors together in surprising new ways, working through comparisons and contrasts, close reading, and playful questioning.

The course begins by exploring the differences between artful reading and everyday reading. How, we ask, does reading a short story or novel differ from reading a memo, a recipe, or a newspaper? How does it differ from other kinds of serious reading? Can you approach a biography or a work of history in the same way that you approach a work of fiction—and if not, why not?

In the opening lecture, and throughout the entire course, we challenge two common misconceptions: first, that smart, sensitive readers are born, not made; and second, that sophistication and intelligence are the sworn enemies of pleasure and delight. From start to finish, it should be clear that the art of reading can be taught—and that mastering this art is both exciting and rewarding.

After defining the art of reading, we examine the figure of the author. How much do we need to know about an author before we can begin to appreciate her work? How do authors approach the task of writing? Do they begin with big themes and big ideas—or with characters, situations, and images? Why are so many authors surprised by their own creations? Should a writer not know how the story will come out?

©2009 The Teaching Company.

Building on such questions, we shift our attention from the author to the narrator or storyteller. (We will also see why we should not confuse the author with the narrator.) We may remember the difference between first- and third-person narrators, but we probably have not considered the larger implications of these devices. What are the advantages and disadvantages of each approach? Why would an author use multiple narrators or create a narrator who seems inadequate or dishonest?

As we refine our questions and explore the most basic elements of storytelling—characterization, description, style; the use of irony and ambiguity—we shift our focus to the crucial issue of narrative structure. In these lectures, we consider two different theories of plot and plotting, contrasting the views of Aristotle with those of the Russian formalists. Later lectures deepen our understanding of plot and plotting. It has been said, for example, that there are really only two master plots—"the hero takes a journey" and "a stranger comes to town." Can that possibly be true? And why, in any case, do those two basic plots continue to fascinate and satisfy us?

As we wrap up the first half of the course, we apply our new insights to a set of increasingly complex examples. A lecture on the Sherlock Holmes stories prepares us for a discussion of *Ivanhoe* and *Jane Eyre*, and that discussion in turn gets us ready for an encounter with modernist masterpieces by Faulkner and Woolf. We will see that our new understanding of the art of reading can help us to make better sense of books that might once have seemed forbidding—and deepen our enjoyment of more familiar works.

The second half of the course introduces the other major building blocks of fiction: chapters, scenes and summaries, subtext, and dialogue. This part of the course also features a lecture on cinematic adaptation, taking off from the familiar and often justified complaint that the movie is never quite as good as the book. As these lectures unfold, we also consider the rise of highly self-conscious fiction, often called metafiction, focusing on the delightful examples of Jorge Luis Borges and Italo Calvino.

These later lectures complicate our sense of what it means to read closely and carefully. Indeed, these lectures will confront us with a number of important theoretical and philosophical questions. Should we expect every work of fiction to be realistic? And what do we mean by "realism," anyway? What is the role of the reader? How are

©2009 The Teaching Company.

readers affected by their encounters with fictional characters? To what extent are readers merely passive observers, and to what extent are they active participants in the production of literary meaning?

As the second half of the course nears its end, we take up a second series of increasingly challenging examples, beginning with a contemporary short story (Alice Munro's "Runaway"), moving on to a classic novel celebrated for its emotional restraint (Edith Wharton's *The Age of Innocence*), and closing with a work notorious for its narrative excesses (Leo Tolstoy's *War and Peace*). By examining works of increasing length and complexity, we see how the most basic narrative structures and literary devices can be employed, extended, and elaborated. In our discussion of each example, we also give close, careful attention to small details—shifts in tone, modulations of voice, the selection and arrangement of words—noting their contribution to the work as a whole.

Thus, although this course raises many complex issues, its largest aim is its simplest and most enduring: to enhance our enjoyment of literature by making us better, more sensitive, and thus more artful readers.

Lecture One
Artful Reading and Everyday Reading

Scope:

This introductory lecture will take on the questions raised by our title: Is there any such thing as an "art of reading"? Isn't reading a practical skill, something most of us master in grade school? If you know the words and can make sense of the sentences, what more do you really need to do? To answer such questions, we will need to take a brief look at the history and science of reading. Then we will explore the many differences between artful reading and everyday reading. In this lecture, then, and throughout the rest of the course, we will learn that it is never too late to begin reading well and discover what generations of book lovers have always know: Artful readers have more fun.

Outline

I. We begin by taking a close look at the phrase that will lie at the heart of these lectures: "the art of reading."

    A. What exactly do we mean by that phrase?

    B. In developing this thought, I would offer three initial points.

        1. First, when you think about reading as an art, you begin to take it a little more seriously.

        2. Second, the idea of artful reading may suggest that there is a difference between reading and reading well.

        3. Finally, the idea of artful reading suggests that you are doing something for its own sake. This sort of reading is its own reward.

    C. In the end, our reservations about the art of reading should give way to a sense of possibility and potential.

II. Having offered an initial comment on the idea of artful reading, I extend my argument in a couple of directions.

    A. First, note that the act of learning to read is no simple matter.

    B. Second, there is a difference between artful reading and what we might call everyday reading.

        1. In everyday reading, your goal is simply to extract information.

©2009 The Teaching Company.

  2. Artful reading is what you do with a work of fiction—when you stop to take note of an elegant phrase or a striking image.

III. So what, then, are the goals of our course?

 A. To make sure that everyday reading is not the only kind of reading we can do.

 B. To give ourselves the chance to read in ways that go beyond extraction and disposal.

 C. To discover what generations of book lovers have always known—that artful readers have more fun.

IV. Having laid out our goals, we are ready to talk about the contents and methods of the course.

 A. We start with the contents.

  1. Our British authors will include many of my all-time favorites: Jane Austen, Charles Dickens, Thomas Hardy, and Virginia Woolf, to name just a few.

  2. Our American writers will include Edgar Allan Poe, Nathaniel Hawthorne, Ernest Hemingway, William Faulkner, and F. Scott Fitzgerald.

  3. Finally, in addition to our selections from the United States and the United Kingdom, we will look at a few writers from other parts of the world.

  4. In addition to classics, we will look at contemporary works.

 B. My goal in assembling these materials is twofold.

  1. First, I want you to be aware of how much great stuff there is out there—and how much great stuff is still being produced today.

  2. In addition, I want you to feel confident of your ability to read, enjoy, and appreciate almost any book that comes your way.

 C. What is the method?

  1. For our purposes, the best approach is likely to be a formalist approach.

  2. When you take a formalist approach, you tend to focus more on questions of form or technique.

  3. Like all committed formalists, we will do a lot of close reading, or giving close, careful attention to the words on the page.

V. Now for the organization of our course: How will the lectures be arranged?

   A. Our first few lectures will familiarize us with various elements of fiction.

   B. In Lectures Ten, Eleven, and Twelve, we will see how all of the elements come together in particular works of fiction, and we will make the transition from short stories to novels.

   C. In the second part of our course—Lectures Thirteen to Twenty-Four—we will move in a similar way.

   1. We will begin with a lecture on chapters.

   2. Then we will move on to lectures on a number of closely related topics: the use of scene and summary, the importance of subtexts, and the role of dialogue.

   3. Later in this sequence, we will turn to some larger questions about reading.

VI. People often ask me why they cannot just read for fun.

   A. When they do, I like to tell them that although I am an English teacher, I have nothing against fun.

   B. Indeed, my aim is to expand your definition of fun, to show that it can include thinking and talking—not to mention reading, reading, and more reading!

Suggested Reading:

Lewis, *An Experiment in Criticism.*

Wolf, *Proust and the Squid.*

Questions to Consider:

1. What are your initial reactions to a phrase like "the art of reading"? If reading can be artful, then what about listening to music or looking at a painting?

2. Do you feel obligated to finish every book you start? If so, what keeps you going? How often are you pleasantly surprised? How often do you find that an unpromising book turns out to be a pretty good read?

©2009 The Teaching Company.

Lecture One—Transcript
Artful Reading and Everyday Reading

Hello, and welcome to Lecture One in our course on the "art of reading."

My name is Tim Spurgin, and it'll be my pleasure to take you through this course.

In this introductory lecture, I'll try to accomplish several things. I'd like to lay out the goals of the course, sketch the contents of the course, and say a bit about the methods of the course.

I'll also do what I can to suggest that the course will be fun. My experience as a teacher has convinced me that people learn best when they're enjoying themselves. It's my hope that a playful and occasionally irreverent approach will pay big dividends for us in the end.

So, let's begin by taking a close look at the phrase that will lie at the heart of these lectures.

I'm talking, of course, about the art of reading. What exactly do we mean by that phrase? Is there really any such thing as the art of reading? If so, are ordinary people—people with demanding jobs and busy lives—really capable of mastering it?

These are not trivial questions. For our phrase is one that may inspire conflicting, even contradictory, responses.

On the one hand, you may feel intimidated by a phrase like the art of reading. You may enjoy nothing more than curling up with a good book—and still be convinced that you lack the ambition, or the talent, or the experience to read "artfully."

On the other hand, you may be put off by the phrase. It may even strike you as a little pretentious: Painters, composers, choreographers, architects—those people practice an art. Readers, viewers, listeners—they do something else. So, let's not go overboard here. Let's not confuse them with the real artists.

Both of those responses make some sense to me.

Still, I don't think that we should be too quick to dismiss the notion of "artful reading." In developing that thought, I would offer three initial points.

First, when you think about reading as an art, you begin to take it a little more seriously. You begin to feel that it's something you shouldn't try to do while watching the game or waiting for the bus.

Second, the idea of artful reading may suggest that there's a difference between reading and reading well—a difference between getting through a book and really getting something out of it. So, if you've always enjoyed reading, but have also thought you might benefit from some coaching or direction, a course on the art of reading might be just the thing for you.

Finally, the idea of artful reading suggests that you're doing something for its own sake—not because it'll make you more popular, and not because it'll help you to get ahead at work; not even because it'll help you to invest more wisely, or lose weight, or lower your cholesterol. No. This sort of reading is its own reward.

So, in the end, our reservations about the art of reading should give way to a sense of possibility and potential. Wouldn't it be great if you could learn to read not just capably, and not just competently, but "artfully"? Wouldn't it be great if you developed the skills and the confidence you'd need to enjoy and appreciate even the most demanding authors?

I think it would be great, and I also believe that it's well within your reach. I won't try to convince you that it will always be fast and easy—but I don't want to make it sound like training for a marathon, either. This is something you can do, and (as I suggested earlier) something you will enjoy doing.

Having offered an initial comment on the idea of artful reading, I might go on to extend my argument in a couple of directions.

First, I might note that the act of learning to read is no simple matter. As Maryanne Wolf, a professor of child development, puts it in her book, *Proust and the Squid*: "We were never born to read."

What does she mean by that? For starters, she means that reading is actually a fairly recent development in human history—something we came up with only a few thousand years ago. So, humans don't seem to need reading and writing in the way that they need, say, language or speech.

In addition, Wolf is pointing to the fact that learning to read appears to result in a kind of rewiring or reprogramming of the brain itself.

 ©2009 The Teaching Company.

As she develops this idea, she offers a really fascinating detail—namely, that the neuronal connections used in reading one language (like Chinese) are different from those used in reading other languages (like English or French).

If that's true—and there's no reason to doubt it—we may find further justification for thinking that "artful readers" are made—and not born. Perhaps learning to read is not something you accomplish in the first or second grade. Perhaps it's a complex process that can extend well into adult life.

(I'm not attributing this view to Professor Wolf, mind you—just suggesting that her work gives us reason to suspect that artful reading doesn't come naturally. Like any other sort of reading, it's the result of training and experience.)

The second point to make here is that there's a difference between "artful reading" and what we might call "everyday reading."

Everyday reading is what you do with a recipe, or a memo, or an e-mail, or an instruction manual. When you do that sort of reading, your goal is simply to extract information. What ingredients go into this lasagna? What time is the meeting? What do I do with the leftover parts for my kid's swingset?

Once you've made that extraction—and once you've gotten the information—you really have no further use for the message. You might keep it as an aid to your memory, but you won't go back to it for any other reason.

We do lots, and lots, and lots of this sort of reading. Really, I think we read most newspapers and magazines in the very same way. First, we extract the information, and then we discard the message—stuffing today's paper or this week's issue into the recycling bin.

As I say, artful reading—that's completely different. Artful reading is what you do with a work of fiction—with a novel or a short story. It's what you do when you stop to take note of an elegant phrase or a striking image.

It's what you do when you ask what it might be like to lose your faith at age 14, or experience shellshock, or discover that your husband is having an affair with one of your best friends.

(And by the way, those examples aren't chosen at random. You'll encounter all of those situations as we make our way through the first part of our course.)

Artful reading might also be associated with rereading—going back over a sentence or a paragraph just to savor its beauty; returning to a story or a novel just to reconnect with those characters.

So, we've got everyday reading and artful reading: extracting information and taking pleasure in language—discarding the original message and returning to it again and again.

I hope that helps you to get an initial sense of our goals and purposes. Before wrapping up our discussion of those goals, I'd like to offer the first in a long list of book recommendations.

If you're really interested in reading about reading, you will enjoy a book called *An Experiment in Criticism* by C. S. Lewis. (Yes, that's the same C. S. Lewis who wrote *The Chronicles of Narnia* and *The Screwtape Letters*.)

In the opening chapters of this book, Lewis offers his own version of the distinction between everyday reading and artful reading. For him, there are several traits or qualities shared by most devoted readers.

He says, for example, that devoted readers are willing—and sometimes eager—to read things more than once. (We've already touched on this point ourselves, right?)

Lewis says that for devoted readers, books aren't a last resort—something you pick up when there's nothing better to do. He adds that devoted readers may experience their encounters with certain books as "momentous" and life-changing experiences.

At this point, I should probably explain that although I will occasionally describe the benefits of rereading, as Lewis does, I won't assume that it's absolutely necessary.

Indeed, I'll try to help you make your first reading more like a second or even a third reading. That's because I want you to be confident of your ability to "get it"—most of it, at least—on your first time through.

I should probably also explain that, in my mind, the question is not how much or even how often you read. What matters is what you bring to your reading and what you try to take away from it.

©2009 The Teaching Company.

Do you approach a new book with a feeling of anticipation? When you get a chance to read, do you make the most of that opportunity? I hope that after listening to these lectures, you'll be more likely to say "yes."

Finally, I want to assure you that although I agree with Lewis about the potential of reading to provide a "momentous" experience, I wouldn't want you to expect that kind of experience from every one of the books we discuss. If some of them don't really move or interest you, that's OK with me.

So what, then, are the goals of our course? To make sure that everyday reading is not the only kind of reading we can do; to give ourselves the chance to read in ways that go beyond "extraction" and "disposal." Finally, to discover what generations of book lovers have always known—namely, that artful readers have more fun.

Having laid out our goals, I think we're ready to talk about the contents and methods of the course.

Let's start with the contents. It's obvious that we'll need to look at lots and lots of examples. So where will those examples come from? Which writers and which works will occupy our attention?

To be honest, the list is too long for me to recite in full. I will tell you, however, that it includes writers from both sides of the Atlantic. Our British authors will include many of my all-time favorites: Jane Austen, Charles Dickens, Thomas Hardy, Virginia Woolf, to name just a few.

What about American writers? Which of them will we get to know? For starters, Edgar Allan Poe and Nathaniel Hawthorne, Ernest Hemingway, William Faulkner, and F. Scott Fitzgerald.

Finally, in addition to our selections from the U.S. and U.K., we'll look at a few writers from other parts of the world: Anton Chekhov and Leo Tolstoy from Russia, Jorge Luis Borges from Argentina, and Italo Calvino from Italy.

Are we confining ourselves to classic works? No. In addition to familiar titles—*Ivanhoe*, *The Age of Innocence*—we'll be looking at contemporary works by authors like Jhumpa Lahiri and Alice Munro. We'll even have a thing or two to say about Harry Potter!

My goal in assembling these materials is twofold. First, I want you to be aware of how much great stuff there is out there—and how much great stuff is still being produced today. I like the classics as much as anyone—most of my teaching is focused in the 19th century—but I also want you to know something about the art of your own time. Even in the midst of cable TV, and videogames, and the Internet—literary fiction remains alive and well.

In addition, I want you to feel confident of your ability to read, enjoy, and appreciate almost any book that comes your way. Whether it's a page-turner like *The Adventures of Sherlock Holmes* or a "metafictional" experiment like *If on a Winter's Night a Traveler*, I hope you'll be ready to take the plunge.

One last thing here—and it may come as something of a surprise. I hope you'll feel free, if you're just not connecting with a work, to set it aside and move on to something else. Reading should be a pleasure, not a chore or a burden. That's how I see it, anyway.

I should tell you that in discussing this issue with folks from The Teaching Company, I've been introduced to what we might call the "50-page test." Let me tell you how it works.

When you pick up a new book, you give yourself permission to drop it after 50 pages. In the meantime, you'll do your best. You won't let yourself make snap judgments about the characters or their actions. You won't assume that you just can't get it—or won't ever understand it.

After all, lots of books start out by plunging you into confusion. That's a very common approach to storytelling. So it would be a mistake to assume that the confusion you may be feeling on page 1, 2, or 3 will still be with you on page 45 or 50.

Still, if you get to page 50 and you're not sure the book is for you—maybe it's hard for you to relate to the characters, or maybe the situation hits too close to home—please, by all means, feel free to put it down. By that point, your conscience should be clear.

Still, it's also worth remembering that most hard-core readers have had the experience of going back to a book they once discarded—and finding that it's terrific. You didn't think you'd ever be able to finish this one, and now (for whatever reason) you find that you just can't put it down.

©2009 The Teaching Company.

The reasons for that are many. The first time around, you were distracted. Or maybe you were trying to read it in little dribs and drabs before going to bed. Or maybe, just maybe, some teacher or professor spoiled it for you.

Nothing makes me happier than to hear that someone has decided to give a great book a second chance. So, let's say that if I give you permission to apply the "50-page test," you will promise me to take a second look at some of the books on your own personal discard pile.

So, if those are the contents, then what are the methods? How will we try to accomplish our goals?

There are many methods to choose from here, and that makes this question a tricky one. We could take a Marxist or a psychoanalytic approach. We could view our works from a feminist or a postcolonial perspective—looking to see what they had to say about issues of gender, race, national identity, or ethnicity.

All of those approaches would be useful and productive. But for our purposes, the best approach is likely to be a formalist approach. When you take a formalist approach, you tend to focus less on broad themes (love, death, identity, justice) and more on questions of form or technique.

So, a formalist might ask: "Why is this story told in the first person?" Or, "How is this character introduced to the reader?" Or, "Why aren't the events of this story presented in chronological order?"

Please don't get me wrong. Most scholars use a variety of approaches: a little bit from Marx, a little bit from Freud, a little bit of feminism—and, when you get right down to it, a whole lot of formalism. Even the most exotic approaches to literary interpretation rely on formalist questions and formalist methods. So, formalism— it's a great place for us to start and a very, very good approach for us to be taking.

Like all committed formalists, we'll do a lot of "close reading." Maybe you've heard that phrase before, and maybe you haven't. But either way, you shouldn't find it difficult to understand.

Because all we really have in mind when we talk about close reading is giving close, careful attention to the words on the page. Are those words casual or refined? Are they familiar or unfamiliar?

Going further—does the language stay the same from start to finish? Or is there some sort of movement or modulation—a shift into a different register or a different key?

Finally, what feelings might lie behind the choice and the arrangement of those words? Are those feelings obvious or obscure? Are they right on the surface, or have they been disguised or hidden in some way?

I hope those questions sound provocative—maybe even tantalizing. But I also want to give you a concrete sense of what I have in mind. So, in the next few minutes, I'm going to offer close readings of the opening passages from two classic works of American literature.

The first passage comes from *The Adventures of Huckleberry Finn*, published by Sam Clemens (a.k.a. Mark Twain) in the middle of the 1880s. Here's how that goes:

> You don't know about me, without you have read a book by the name of "The Adventures of Tom Sawyer," but that ain't no matter. That book was made by Mr. Mark Twain, and he told the truth, mainly. There was things which he stretched, but mainly he told the truth. That is nothing. I never seen anybody but lied, one time or another, without it was Aunt Polly, or the widow, or maybe Mary. Aunt Polly—Tom's Aunt Polly, she is—and Mary, and the Widow Douglas, is all told about in that book—which is mostly a true book, with some stretchers, as I said before.

Many of you have probably read that before—maybe more than once. (*Huck Finn* remains a standard offering in most U.S. lit courses.) But how closely have you read it? What might a close reading reveal to you? Those are the real questions for us.

It seems to me that if you focus your attention on the words themselves—not the larger themes of truth-telling and lying, but the actual words themselves—you start to see lots of things you wouldn't expect to find in a great work of literature.

Like what? Well, the passage is full of slang expressions. It includes non-standard words like "ain't" and ungrammatical constructions like "There was things" and "I never seen."

So what can we take away from that? Quite a bit, for in addition to raising questions of truth and falsehood—I don't think we want to dismiss those questions entirely—this paragraph means to expand our sense of what a book can be.

What does the paragraph tell us? For starters, it tells us that books don't have to be civilized. They can be rough, and raw, and maybe even a little clumsy, because those qualities won't necessarily interfere with their intelligence or their integrity.

Before we go on, we have to recognize another important fact: This passage is not really the work of a marginally literate boy, but rather a simulation or imitation of such a work. Its roughness, and rawness, and clumsiness are deliberate, not accidental—and as such, they're probably meant to kick our imaginations into high gear from the start. Why write in this voice? Why write in this way? *Tom Sawyer* isn't told in the first person. So, if this book is an offshoot of that one, why should it be so different?

That's an awful lot to get out of the first paragraph, I know. But I think it's all there. In fact, I think there's even more there. What are we to make, for example, of the fact that Huck associates men (including Mark Twain) with lying, and women (Aunt Polly, and the widow, and maybe Mary) with honesty? What are we to make, moreover, of that crucial word "maybe"? What about the closely related word, "mainly"—as in "he told the truth, mainly"?

To get an even better sense of how this paragraph comes together, we might consider an alternative version of the paragraph—one told by an outside, or "third-person," narrator. Let's assume, just for the fun of it, that this new narrator is determined to speak correctly—maybe even elegantly. Here's what that might sound like:

> Though you will not recognize the characters portrayed in this work if you are unfamiliar with the author's earlier depiction of them in *The Adventures of Tom Sawyer*, that is no cause for concern. Indeed, it is worth noting that *Tom Sawyer* contains more than its fair share of exaggeration and distortion, despite the author's best efforts to report the facts honestly.

See the difference there? Right away, the whole thing has a completely different feel: same themes—honesty, deception, storytelling—but a completely different feel. Why? In large part because we're now looking down on Tom and Huck—and we're already assuming that only one kind of language, a highly formal and elaborate language, is appropriate for serious writing.

We could explore all of that further—but I'd rather leave you wanting more. Besides, we have another passage to consider.

This one comes from *The Turn of the Screw* by Henry James—a classic ghost story published in the 1890s. Here's how it starts:

> The story had held us, round the fire, sufficiently breathless, but except the obvious remark that it was gruesome, as on Christmas Eve in an old house a strange tale should essentially be, I remember no comment uttered till somebody happened to note it as the only case he had met in which such a visitation had fallen on a child.

As you may have noticed, that's all just one long sentence. But even so, it'll give us more than enough to work with.

Here, it's clear that we're dealing with a highly skilled writer—a person who chooses and arranges his words with great care—the opposite of *Huck Finn* in other words. This person, James's narrator, is also the sort of person who knows how to create dramatic effects. He saves the most powerful words in the sentence (namely, "visitation" and "child") for the very end. He makes his way to those two words slowly and deliberately—so that when he gets there, the words have an even more disturbing or startling effect.

Looking at the end of the sentence might make an artful reader flash back to the beginning, where she'll find another key word: "story." Once she sees that word, she knows that this long and seemingly effortless sentence is meant to arc, ever so gracefully, from "story" down to "visitation" and "child."

So what has been revealed by this little bit of close reading? For starters, that this, *The Turn of the Screw*, is a story about storytelling—and that this story will generate suspense through the juxtaposition of opposites: "gruesome" and "Christmas Eve"; "visitation" and "child."

In talking about *Huck Finn*, we began to learn one very important lesson: namely, that the words on the page might well have been different.

Can we play the same game with this passage? Can we imagine an alternate version of what we're getting from Henry James?

 ©2009 The Teaching Company.

Of course—what happens, for example, if we make the sentence shorter? What happens if, instead of saving the word "child" for the very end, we stick it somewhere in the middle?

Here's how that might sound: "The story of the gruesome visitation to the child, told to us in an old house on Christmas Eve, had held us breathless."

Once again, we've retained all of the original themes and most of the original words, too—yet, as in the case of our revisions to *Huck Finn*, the feeling is entirely different. For one thing, we've lost any sense of the narrator's personality. He no longer seems to delight in his use of language. He no longer takes great pleasure in leading us up to the creepiest, most unusual elements of this particular ghost story.

Once you see the power of close reading, you may be inspired to ask lots of other questions? Why should the narrator have heard this story on Christmas Eve? (It could just as easily have been New Year's Eve, right?) Who was with him, sitting around that fire, when he first heard it? Who, most urgently, was the original storyteller? Who told the story to him? Is this something he heard from a reliable source, or is it the 19th-century equivalent of an "urban legend"?

That's probably enough for now, though. With the time we've got left, I'd like to offer a few more general points.

Point number one: Close reading skills are very, very useful. As we've seen, they can be applied to works by authors as different as Mark Twain and Henry James. (And believe me, it's hard to imagine authors as different as those two!)

Point number two: Close reading skills almost always take us back to the words on the page. When you're reading through a book, it's easy to speculate about all sorts of things. What is the meaning of life? Why do we have to die? How do we know what's right and what's wrong? Believe me, that's OK. That's one of the things that reading is supposed to do for us.

Even so, it's important to stay grounded—to remember that the writer's medium is language. She achieves all of her effects through words. A painter may work in oil, or acrylic, or watercolors. A composer may write for a great big orchestra or a small ensemble. But all a writer ever has is language—the language we all use every day. Close reading not only reminds us of that fact, but also encourages us to go beyond our everyday uses of language. When we read closely, we enlarge our sense of what words can do.

Of course, that's not all we're doing. For in addition to enlarging our sense of language, we're enlarging our sense of ourselves. How are we like these characters, and how are we different? What do we all have in common, and what makes each of us unique? Finally, how deep or certain is our self-knowledge? Are we capable of seeing ourselves directly, or do we need to view ourselves from a distance or at an angle—as we do when reading a work of fiction?

Point number three (and this is the last one): Close reading is not the only tool in our box. Indeed, I think that one of the most original features of this course is its emphasis on the nuts and bolts of reading: How do you begin a long novel? What do you look for as you're getting started? What kinds of questions should you be asking along the way? When and how do you benefit from rereading?

In just about every lecture, we'll take up such questions. We'll learn about exercises like "prereading." We'll devise some activities that might work especially well for book groups and family reading circles.

So much for methods—as far as I can see, only one thing remains—and that is the organization of our course. How will the lectures be arranged? What will come first? What will come after that?

Our first few lectures will familiarize us with various elements of fiction: narration, characterization, description, and so forth. We'll take those elements one by one, making sure that we know what each of them can contribute to our experience of reading.

Through these lectures, we'll deal mainly with short stories rather than full-length novels. That approach will help us to build confidence quickly. Besides, short stories make for great reading—especially if you're pressed for time.

Before long—in Lectures Ten, Eleven, and Twelve—we'll see how all of the elements come together in particular works of fiction. In these lectures, we will make the transition from short stories to novels—closing our sequence with two brilliant examples of modernist experimentation: *As I Lay Dying* by William Faulkner, and *The Waves* by Virginia Woolf.

In the second part of our course—Lectures Thirteen to Twenty-Four—we'll move in a similar way. We'll begin with a lecture on

©2009 The Teaching Company.

chapters. Then, we'll move on to lectures on a number of closely related topics: the use of "scene" and "summary," the importance of "subtexts," the role of dialogue.

Later in this sequence, we'll turn to some larger questions about reading. What is the role of the reader? Is she a passive receiver of meanings, or is she an active creator of them?

What do we mean by "realism"? Is there more than one way for a book to be realistic?

Finally, how come the movie is never as good as the book? What usually gets left out in the complicated process of adaptation?

This part of the course will end, as the first part did, with a series of increasingly complicated examples—culminating with Tolstoy's *War and Peace*, one of the most daunting—and most enjoyable— works of fiction ever written.

That does it, then. Those are the goals, the contents, the methods, and the organization of our course. None of it will make any difference without you, of course, and so I'll just remind you of my hope that this will be a pleasure for us both.

People often ask me why they can't just read for fun. When they do, I like to tell them that although I'm an English teacher, I have nothing against fun. I'm not anti-fun. Indeed, my aim is to expand your definition of fun, to show that it can include thinking and talking—not to mention reading, reading, and more reading.

Thank you very much for joining us. We'll look forward to seeing you soon.

Lecture Two
Authors, Real and Implied

Scope:

When reading a good book, we seem to be in touch with another person. This person, the author, appears to speak to us directly. He anticipates our questions, keeps us in suspense, and eventually satisfies our expectations—and all he asks in return is that we keep turning the pages. But are such relationships really so simple? How much can we learn about an author from his books? And how, finally, should we understand our relationship with the author—who may be long dead, and who in any case knows next to nothing about us? Such questions will be a springboard for this lecture, helping us to see how the intelligent, artful reader conceives of the complex and contradictory figure of the author.

Outline

I. I have had a chance to meet a few authors, and I can tell you that the experience is often thrilling; however, sometimes it can be very disappointing.

   A. Here are some of the questions we want to address here.
       1. How do we get to know an author?
       2. What is the relationship between the person we think we know from the books and the real-life person we might meet?
       3. What do authors have to say about authorship?

   B. Here is our plan.
       1. We will start with a passage from a familiar story.
       2. Then we will explore the ideas of two literary theorists.
       3. Finally, we will see what authors typically have to say about the creative process.

   C. A couple of ideas will be important throughout.
       1. The possibility that authors are in some ways more like characters than creators.
       2. Writers almost never begin with a theme or a message.

 ©2009 The Teaching Company.

II. Our first example is the opening paragraph of *A Christmas Carol* by Charles Dickens.

    A. You might already notice a few things about Dickens's writing.

        1. The figure materializing before you is a storyteller and, perhaps, also an entertainer.

        2. This figure wants you to ask questions.

        3. This figure also wants you to see that he loves his job.

    B. If we read on, it is not only to find out more about Marley and Scrooge—it is to deepen our relationship, our connection, to this author.

    C. I advise readers to think about the author not as a creator but rather as a character.

    D. What we see here is what we will be seeing throughout the course.

        1. There is more to reading fiction than simply extracting information.

        2. There is more to it than simply meeting the characters and following the story to its conclusion.

III. In the second part of this lecture, we consider the ideas of two influential critics. The first is T. S. Eliot.

    A. Eliot argues that the author's personality is largely irrelevant to the production of her work.

    B. He advanced these claims in "Tradition and the Individual Talent."

    C. In this essay, Eliot sets up a contrast between the "man who suffers" and the "mind that creates."

        1. The "man who suffers" is the person who goes to the grocery store and the gym.

        2. The "mind that creates" is the mind that drives and shapes and inhabits the writing itself.

    D. Eliot's ideas are reassuring and helpful. They give us a way to enjoy the books without expecting too much of the real-life author.

IV. The second theorist is Wayne C. Booth.

    A. In his classic study, *The Rhetoric of Fiction*, Booth extends and refines some of Eliot's thinking on the subject of authorship.

B. Booth is interested in the contrast between the real-life author and the "implied author."

    1. The implied author is the figure who materializes in the book itself, the man or woman whose personality is implicit in the story and the storytelling.

    2. Booth's very deliberate use of the word "implied" suggests that his real concern is with what the author leaves unspoken or unsaid.

V. Just as the artful reader understands the difference between the implied author and flesh-and-blood author, he or she understands that authors do not necessarily begin with a theme or message.

VI. We conclude with the next-to-last paragraph in Dickens's most famous story.

A. It contains seven repetitions of the word "good," and it also distinguishes between two different forms of laughter.

B. Dickens was not always able to live that way himself, but what matters is the words on the page, the figure or character of the storyteller, and the spirit or feeling he inspires in us.

C. The message of *A Christmas Carol*, though admirable, is not really all that special. What we will never tire of hearing, though, is the voice of this storyteller—or, if you like, this implied author.

Suggested Reading:

Booth, *The Rhetoric of Fiction*, chaps. 3, 6.

The Paris Review, *The Paris Review Interviews*.

Questions to Consider:

1. If you could get your favorite writers on the phone, what would you want to ask them?

2. Are you surprised to hear writers like Morrison and Faulkner describe the creative process as one of discovery? Do you believe them when they say that they tend not to start with a message or moral?

Lecture Two—Transcript
Authors, Real and Implied

Hello, and welcome to Lecture Two in our course on the "art of reading." In our first lecture, we began to talk about the reader, and we had lots and lots of questions. What kind of reader do you want to be? What's the difference between artful reading and everyday reading? In this lecture, and in the two that follow it, we'll consider the reader's encounters with several other figures. First comes the author, and then the narrator, and finally the characters. That makes sense—because with each of those steps, we'll move deeper and deeper into the story itself.

So, authors. I have had a chance to meet a few of them, and I can tell you that the experience is often thrilling. It's great to be in the presence of people like John Updike, Salman Rushdie, or Jane Hamilton. Here, I have to make a confession. I pretty much fell in love with Jane Hamilton instantaneously. She is kind, and smart—and so, so funny. So, if you haven't read *The Book of Ruth*, or *The Map of the World*, you should. If you ever get a chance to hear Jane read from her works aloud, you really have to do that too.

Sometimes, it's no fun to meet the author. Sometimes, in fact, it can be very disappointing. The person who had seemed so wise—and, let's face it, so wonderful—sometimes turns out to be a great big jerk. Obviously, I can't name names here. When that sort of thing happens, should we really be surprised? More importantly, should we even care? I mean, so what if an author turns out to be vain, or boring, or mean? Does that have to spoil everything for us as readers?

Those are good questions—and we'll often return to them in this lecture. But they aren't the only questions we'll need to ask. So before we do anything else, let's run down some of the other questions we'll want to address here.

First: How do we get to know an author? How does the figure of the author make his presence known to us? How does that figure first begin to materialize on the page?

Second, what is the relationship between the person we think we know from the books and the real-life person we might meet at a reading or a book festival? How much do we really need to know about the real-life person in order to understand or enjoy the books?

Is it a help or a hindrance to know, let's say, that such-and-such a character was based on the author's father, or ex-husband, or brother-in-law?

Finally: What do authors have to say about authorship? How do they understand the larger creative process?

Those are our questions, then. Now here's our plan. We'll start with a passage from a very familiar story. (Let's keep the title a secret for now.) Then, we'll explore the ideas of two prominent literary theorists. (Don't worry—those ideas will help us to make sense of all this.) Finally, we'll see what authors typically have to say about the creative process. They should know best, right?

A couple of ideas will be important throughout. First, we'll need to consider the possibility that authors are in some ways more like characters than creators. It may be, in other words, that we can only meet them in the pages of our favorite books.

Second—and this may be an even more important point: No matter what your teachers or your professors may have told you, writers almost never begin with a theme or a message. When they talk about writing, they do not present themselves as all-knowing, all-seeing masterminds. Instead, they speak of asking questions, exploring new possibilities, and losing control.

With all of that in mind, let's turn to that first juicy example.

"Marley was dead: to begin with." Does that sound familiar? If not, don't worry—because it will.

> Marley was dead: to begin with. There is no doubt whatever about that. The register of his burial was signed by the clergyman, the clerk, the undertaker, and the chief mourner. Scrooge signed it: and Scrooge's name was good upon 'Change, for anything he chose to put his hand to. Old Marley was as dead as a door-nail.

This is, of course, the opening paragraph of *A Christmas Carol* by Charles Dickens. Although we haven't gotten very far, you might already notice a few things about Dickens's writing. First, he isn't offering to teach you the true meaning of Christmas. That's what people always say about the *Christmas Carol*: It teaches you the true meaning of Christmas. In this passage, Dickens isn't offering to teach you anything.

 ©2009 The Teaching Company.

The figure materializing before you is not a teacher—but rather a storyteller and, perhaps, also an entertainer. This figure wants you to ask questions: So, who is Marley? Are we supposed to know who he is, recognize that name? How did he die? Why would anyone have any doubts about his passing?

This figure also wants you to see that he loves his job. He's excited to be with us—there is a lot of energy in this writing—and he wants us to share in his delight. In many ways, he seems to be the main attraction here. He is definitely the star of the show. If we read on, it's not only to find out more about Marley and Scrooge—it's to deepen our relationship, our connection, to this author.

Already, I hope you can see why I advise curious readers to think about the author not as a creator, but rather as a sort of character: a figure who materializes on the page; a figure whose image emerges over the course of the story; a figure revealed to us in the language and really in the structure of the work itself.

Fair enough, you might say. But how can we really begin to do that? How might this advice change or influence our approach to reading?

For starters, you might get in the habit of stopping to gather some initial impressions of the author. What sort of person do we seem to be dealing with here? How does this person present himself to us? What are his most striking qualities?

Is he, for example, friendly or chilly? Is he generous or judgmental? Does he have a sense of humor? If so, is it sharp and biting or generous and gentle?

After reading on for another few pages, you might stop to see what else you've noticed. As before, you might ask yourself some questions: What kind of person might write this sort of story or be drawn to these sorts of characters? What does this author seem to want or expect from his readers? Is his aim to entertain, to instruct, or to combine those two things in some way?

What we're seeing here, I hope, is what we'll be seeing throughout the course: There's more to reading fiction than simply extracting information—and more to it than simply meeting the characters and following the story to its conclusion.

To see how much more there can be, let's return to Dickens. We were considering our initial responses to his self-presentation in *A*

Christmas Carol—noting his energy and enthusiasm. But we failed to notice one thing: He ends that paragraph with a cliché: "Marley was as dead as a door-nail."

Perhaps you did notice that. (I really shouldn't assume that you missed it.) If so, you may also have wondered why Dickens would do such a thing. Shouldn't a great author try for something a little more original than "dead as a door-nail"?

As it turns out, Dickens is already one step ahead of us. He wants us to question his use of that cliché—because he's planning to make a joke of it in the very next paragraph. Here's how that goes:

> Mind! [he says] I don't mean to say that I know, of my own knowledge, what there is particularly dead about a door-nail. I might have been inclined, myself, to regard a coffin-nail as the deadest piece of ironmongery in the trade. But the wisdom of our ancestors is in the simile; and my unhallowed hands shall not disturb it, or the Country's done for. You will therefore permit me to repeat, emphatically, that Marley was as dead as a door-nail.

See how that works? After admitting that he's used a cliché, Dickens pretends that he had no choice in the matter. In the process, he takes advantage of the opportunity to spoof the rhetoric of Burkean conservatives. (You know the type: people who assume that if something is old, if something has been around for a long, long time, even if it doesn't make sense—and even if it never made sense—we had better stick with it. Who are we, after all, to set aside the "wisdom of our ancestors"?)

So here, as in the opening paragraph, Dickens is identifying us, us readers, as his compatriots, his colleagues, his partners. Instead of placing himself on a pedestal, he brings us up to his level. We're all on the same side—he tells us—we're all in on the same jokes. In addition to a wonderful story, then, he's offering much, much more: intimacy, reciprocity, fellowship.

After looking at these wonderful paragraphs, we can see why it's so tempting to imagine the author as some sort of personal friend. Like Dickens, our favorite authors seem to be right there with us. They anticipate our needs and grant our wishes—and they ask only one thing in return: that we keep on reading to the end. It's a great deal.

©2009 The Teaching Company.

The pleasures of getting to know an author are summed up, quite nicely, by Holden Caulfield, the teenage protagonist of J. D. Salinger's *The Catcher in the Rye*. Near the beginning of the novel, Holden speaks for almost all passionate readers when he says:

> What really knocks me out is a book that, when you're all done reading it, you wish the author that wrote it was a terrific friend of yours and you could call him up on the phone whenever you felt like it. That doesn't happen much, though.

It certainly doesn't happen much with Salinger himself, as many critics have noted. Yes, there is a deep irony in the fact that this familiar wish—the wish that our favorite writers might love us as much as we love them—comes from one of the most reclusive men of our age.

Yet—that irony doesn't make the wish go away. We do expect a lot from writers, even if we know we probably shouldn't. We hope that a writer will live up to his image, that he'll be the person—or at least the sort of person—we think we've gotten to know from his books.

In many ways, that makes sense. After all, reading creates a remarkable feeling of intimacy. (We've already begun to see how that happens with Dickens.) When you're done with a book, you may feel that you've invested a lot of yourself in it. You've shut yourself off from the rest of the world. You've ignored (or tried to ignore) the phone, the kids, the dog. You've tried to give the author your full attention—and a good bit of your precious time.

So why shouldn't you be disappointed to learn that—in real life—he's nothing like you thought he was? Why shouldn't it be a letdown to discover that he's really a great big jerk?

At this point, we probably need some help sorting things out. (We have definitely made some progress—don't get me wrong—but lots of questions remain.) So, let's turn to the second part of this lecture and consider the ideas of two influential critics.

The first is T. S. Eliot. Eliot is most famous as a poet, of course, but his greatest influence may have come through his critical and theoretical work. His take on the author is both surprising and intriguing.

Eliot insists that it just doesn't matter if a beloved author has feet of clay. He argues that the author's personality is largely irrelevant to the production of her work, and since it doesn't figure into the writing, there's no reason to assume that it should figure into our reading, either.

Eliot advanced these claims in a groundbreaking essay called "Tradition and the Individual Talent," which was published in the 1910s. One of the most interesting moves in the essay comes when Eliot sets up a contrast between the "man who suffers" and the "mind that creates." Because we're going to be using those terms for awhile, I should repeat them: the "man who suffers" and the "mind that creates."

The "man who suffers" is the person who goes to the grocery store and the gym, the one who cashes the checks and pays the bills. This is also the person who may show up on your campus or at your local bookstore—the person who gives a nice, lively reading (or doesn't) and seems happy (or not) to interact with his fans.

The "mind that creates"—now that's something completely different. The "mind that creates" is the mind that drives, and shapes, and inhabits the writing itself. It's responsible for devising the plot, developing the characters, and polishing the sentences and paragraphs.

Here's how Eliot lays out that distinction: "[T]he more perfect the artist [he says] the more completely separate in him will be the man who suffers and the mind which creates; the more perfectly will the mind digest and transmute the passions which are its material."

So, the artist is definitely passionate. He suffers, like the rest of us, and his sufferings may be very keen—very profound. But his passions and suffering don't necessarily make their way onto the page. They get handed over to this other part of the artist—that's the "mind that creates"—for what Eliot calls "digestion" and "transmutation." So, what you get as a reader is not the artist's original feeling—but a rendering or translation of it.

Maybe in the end, then, it doesn't really matter if the author is a jerk. Maybe it's OK if he rushes through his reading or refuses to sign your book—because the part of him that does those things, that's not the part that we care about. Our concern is with the "mind" and not the "man," right?

 ©2009 The Teaching Company.

I think so. Indeed, I believe that Eliot's ideas are reassuring and helpful. They give us a way to enjoy the books without expecting too much of the real-life author.

In sketching this part of the lecture, I suggested that we'd be dealing with the ideas of two prominent theorists. Eliot was the first. So who's the second?

The second theorist is Wayne C. Booth. In his classic study, *The Rhetoric of Fiction*, which he published in the early 1960s, Booth extended and refined some of Eliot's thinking on the subject of authorship. (He also gave us a more useful vocabulary: Eliot's terms—though certainly striking—are also, let's face it, a little cumbersome.)

Booth is interested in the contrast between the "real-life author" and the "implied author." He explains that the "implied author" is the figure who materializes in the book itself, the man or woman whose personality is implicit in the story and the storytelling. This is the person we'd like to befriend—this is the person we wish we could phone, or e-mail, or text, or just hang out with.

In making this point, Booth is offering his version of an idea we considered in our initial discussion of Dickens: Maybe the author—as we know and experience him—is a bit like one of the characters.

At this stage in our discussion, though, we also need to consider Booth's very deliberate use of the word "implied." With that word, Booth suggests that although he's interested in the author's overt or explicit statements, his real concern is with what the author leaves unspoken or unsaid.

So what does this author seem to take for granted? What kind of tale does he usually choose to tell? How far do his sympathies extend? Is he capable of treating all of the characters generously and fairly, or does he play favorites? Does he take cheap shots? Does he score easy points?

These are the sorts of questions Booth likes to ask, and as you've probably noticed, they combine an interest in literary matters with a concern for ethics or morality. Like Holden Caulfield, Booth is alert to the connection between the author and the reader, and he sees it as a kind of friendship. But he doesn't stop there. He wants to know if the author is going to be a good friend. Will this author bring out the best in you, or will he allow you to indulge in some of your worst habits? Will he, in short, be a good influence or a bad one? These questions may never have occurred to you before, and the terms and theories in this lecture may also strike you as new and different. But it seems to me, after talking with all kinds of readers, that this way of thinking is not really so unusual.

Intelligent readers do seem to understand that they shouldn't expect to meet up with their favorite authors at the gym or the supermarket. They know that such meetings can only take place in books, and that's one reason why biographical criticism—especially the kind that looks for exact parallels between the author's life and work—usually strikes them as distracting or pointless.

This is probably a good time for me to tell you that biographical material won't play a very large part in this course. We won't worry about real-life models for beloved characters, or the private sorrows and sufferings of famous authors. Not because those things aren't interesting—but rather because they won't really take us where we want to go. Instead of opening up the chance for further discussion, biographical questions tend to shut it down. To use a sports analogy, they tend to stop the ball dead—instead of moving it down toward the goal line.

This may also be a good time to make an even larger point, one that has been hovering in the background since the beginning of this lecture. Just as the artful reader instinctively understands the difference between the implied author and the flesh-and-blood author, he or she also understands that authors don't necessarily begin with a theme or a message.

I want to be very clear about this point. For although, after years and years of schooling, you may have gotten the idea that the message comes first; you need to know—really, really need to know—that it just doesn't work that way.

Authors do not begin with a message and then look for a way to hide it from you. They aren't speaking in code, and they don't employ symbols or metaphors as a way of testing or tormenting their readers.

What makes me so sure of that? How can I possibly defend these extravagant claims? Perhaps, by looking at what writers have to say about the creative process. How do they describe their efforts? How often do they talk about delivering a message or conveying a moral?

 ©2009 The Teaching Company.

The short answer is: not very often at all. Consider, for example, the statements of Toni Morrison in an interview with *The Paris Review*. Morrison, as you may know, is the author of *The Bluest Eye*, *Sula*, and *Beloved*, among many other classic works. Born in 1931, she was awarded the Nobel Prize in the early 1990s.

Here's what she told the interviewer: "I almost always start out with an idea, even a boring idea, that becomes a question I don't have any answers to."

Let's stop there, noting that ideas play a role in Morisson's process, but those ideas are soon transformed into questions—and not just any questions: questions that she doesn't already have the answers to.

What else does Morrison have to say? Here goes:

> It is not "This is what I believe" [she tells the interviewer] because that would not be a book, just a tract. A book is "This may be what I believe, but suppose I am wrong … what could it be?" Or, "I don't know what it is, but I am interested in finding out what it might mean to me, as well as to other people."

Through all of this, Morrison emphasizes the process of discovery, not the execution of a plan. She also distinguishes books from mere "tracts." In a tract, the author never admits that she may be wrong. She's not interested in seeing how things might look to her readers.

You might hear the same sort of thing from any number of authors—including, for example, William Faulkner. Faulkner is the author of works like *The Sound and the Fury* and *As I Lay Dying*, and he'll figure into our course at several points along the way. Like Morrison, he received the Nobel Prize—and, like her, also sat down for an interview with *The Paris Review*.

Here's what he had to say to the interviewer: "[W]ith me there is always a point in the book where the characters themselves rise up and take charge and finish the job—say somewhere about page 275. Of course I don't know what would happen if I finished the book on page 274."

Notice that for Faulkner, the author is almost a kind of bystander. It's as if he has to be pushed or shoved out of the way. By the time those characters get to page 275, they have had enough of the author!

They're ready to get on with it—to stop dithering and finish the job by themselves.

Interviews are a guilty pleasure of mine. I'm sure you can tell that I just can't get enough of them. The ones from *The Paris Review* are the best. An interview with that magazine is a sign that an author has arrived—it's like a badge of honor—and I'd encourage you not only to look for new issues of *The Paris Review*, but to track down anthologies or collections of those interviews. They're fantastic.

If you do read those interviews, you'll see that these authors don't say much about teaching a lesson, or sending a message, or even making a point. Instead—and I really want to stress this—they talk about asking questions, comparing answers, and waiting to see what happens next. They often speak as if the characters have a life of their own, as if they are simply a kind of medium or conduit through which the characters make their way into our world.

We'll want to keep all of that in mind as we move through the rest of this course. If the creative process is something of a mystery, even to our greatest writers, then perhaps the reading process should possess a bit of that feeling as well. Maybe, instead of looking for a message, or a moral, or a theme, we should let the characters and situations take over—not on page 274, as Faulkner jokes, but from the very start.

That's not the same as reading mindlessly, as I hope I've already begun to make clear. But it's not the same as looking for messages, and morals, and themes, either. In the end, we want to be readers, not codebreakers, and so we must resist the temptation to see the story or the characters as symbols or signs of some deeper, hidden meaning.

The elements of a story may, indeed, point beyond themselves—suggesting some larger truth or raising a profound question. But if the story is any good, they won't do so in an obvious or simple-minded way. Instead, they'll work through suggestions, and implications, and hints. They'll ask us to make guesses and predictions—and to revise our hypotheses as we go. As we learn to do that—and do it more confidently and comfortably—we'll find that we're beginning to master the art of reading.

Let's not close with generalizations, though. Let's conclude instead with another reading from Dickens. This passage should sound familiar too.

©2009 The Teaching Company.

> Scrooge was better than his word. He did it all, and infinitely more; and to Tiny Tim, who did *not* die, he was a second father. He became as good a friend, as good a master, and as good a man, as the good old city knew, or any other good old city, town, or borough, in the good old world. Some people laughed to see the alteration in him, but he let them laugh, and little heeded them; for he was wise enough to know that nothing ever happened on this globe, for good, at which some people did not have their fill of laughter in the outset; and knowing such as these would be blind anyway, he thought it quite as well that they should wrinkle up their eyes in grins, as have the malady in less attractive forms. His own heart laughed: and that was quite enough for him.

That's the next to the last paragraph in Dickens's most famous story, and it contains seven repetitions of the word "good." It also distinguishes between two different forms of laughter. There's a mean or dismissive laughter, like that directed at Scrooge; and then there's a hearty, generous laughter, like that coming from Scrooge. If you can pull off the second form of laughter, Dickens assures us, you won't need to worry about the first.

Unfortunately, Dickens wasn't always able to live that way himself. He was very, very sensitive to criticism—and he did not like to be laughed at. But as I keep trying to say, that's not what really matters here. What matters is the words on the page; the figure or character of the author, the storyteller; and the spirit or feeling he inspires in us.

The message of *A Christmas Carol*, though admirable, is not really all that special. Be kind; keep Christmas in your heart; don't be blind to your own sins. We've heard all of that before, and we'll surely hear it again. What we will never tire of hearing, though, is the voice of this storyteller—or, if you like, this implied author. From start to finish, he invites us to share in his delight. He not only urges us to be more generous, but serves as a model of generosity itself. If we treated others as he treats us, then ours would, indeed, be a good old world.

I think that's enough for now. In our next lecture, we'll build on the foundation we've established here, turning our attention from authors to narrators. Thanks as always for joining us. We'll look forward to seeing you again soon.

Lecture Three
Narrators—Their Voices and Their Visions

Scope:

We begin this lecture with a simple rule: Do not confuse the author with the narrator. Jane Eyre is not Charlotte Brontë, despite the superficial resemblance between them, and Huck Finn is not always a mouthpiece for Mark Twain. As we sort out the distinction between the author and the narrator, we will return to our abiding concern with reading: How does the reader fit into all of this? What does a good reader look for in a narrator? How do we relate to different sorts of narrators? By the end of the lecture, we will see why good readers always pay close attention to the narrator: The choice of a narrator or narrative strategy not only shapes, but actually determines, a host of larger meanings and effects.

Outline

I. We begin with the distinction between first- and third-person narration.

    A. A first-person narrator is an "I" narrator. This type of narrator is one of the characters—a participant or at least a close observer of the action.

    B. A third-person narrator is a "they," "he," or "she" narrator. This sort of narrator tends to stand outside or above the characters, reporting their actions and moving in and out of their minds.

    C. Everyone tells you to remember the difference, but no one tells you why.

    D. There are pros and cons to each kind of narration.

II. We look at examples from two classic American writers: Edgar Allan Poe and Nathaniel Hawthorne.

    A. Poe is most famous for his tales of terror. Almost all of them are told by first-person narrators, and as soon as the narrator starts talking, you just cannot tear yourself away.

    B. We can see one of the big advantages of first-person narration in the opening paragraphs of "The Tell-Tale Heart": It can make a very powerful first impression.

 ©2009 The Teaching Company.

C. The tradition of the first-person narrator goes all the way back to Chaucer.

III. If Poe is drawn to the first-person narrator, then Hawthorne is drawn to the third-person narrator.

    A. Hawthorne actually wants to put some distance between his readers and his characters.

    B. We look at one of Hawthorne's most famous tales: "Young Goodman Brown."

        1. At no point does the narrator explain the point or purpose of Goodman Brown's journey.

        2. As Goodman Brown ventures into the dark forest, he meets some very strange characters; the narrator steadfastly refuses to explain what they are doing.

        3. This narrator gives us the feeling that he knows more than he is letting on. Indeed, he suggests that he may never tell us everything we want to know.

        4. As long as the narrator withholds an explanation, he forces us to consider the possibility that what occurred was not a mirage or a figment of Goodman Brown's imagination—and we begin to get a little uncomfortable.

        5. At the end, the narrator is no longer playful, no longer evasive, and he tells us exactly what happened—in no uncertain terms.

IV. There are some distinct advantages to third-person narration.

    A. With a third-person narrator, there may be a loss of immediacy and intensity—but a writer might want to distance us from the characters.

    B. There are other times when the writer would like to provide some information or insight that is unavailable to the characters themselves.

V. Are there ways to enjoy the advantages of both forms of narration at the same time?

    A. Yes, a third-person narrator can borrow little bits of language from one or more of the characters. Those words do not have to be set off in quotation marks or identified with some sort of tag. This is called free indirect discourse or free indirect style.

B. Free indirect discourse is most closely linked to Gustave Flaubert, as seen in *Madame Bovary*.

C. This form of narration is one of the best and most important.

VI. Is there anything besides first-person, third-person, and free indirect discourse? Yes, there is—though these other possibilities are not nearly as common.

A. It is possible to shift between first- and third-person narrators, as Dickens does in *Bleak House*.

B. It is also possible to shift among several first-person narrators, as Faulkner does in *The Sound and the Fury* and *As I Lay Dying*.

C. It is even possible to create a second-person narrator, a "you" narrator. That is what Lorrie Moore does in some of her early short stories.

D. To extend our survey of unusual narrative possibilities, we might also consider the use of a "we" narrator—that is, a first-person plural narrator.

VII. The choice of a narrator is often crucial to the larger effect of a story.

A. The next time you are 9 or 10 pages into a new book, ask yourself a few simple questions: Is this in first person or third person? How would it be different if it were the other way around?

B. In the end, it is not a simple matter of classifying or categorizing the narrator, but rather a more challenging and rewarding task.

Suggested Reading:

LaPlante, *The Making of a Story*, chap. 6.

Wood, *How Fiction Works*, chaps. 1–2.

Questions to Consider:

1. Do you prefer first-person narratives to third-person narratives? Given a choice between two versions of the same story—one told by a participant and the other told by an outside observer— which would you be more likely to read?

2. In recent years, journalists and biographers have used free indirect discourse to create a stronger sense of what their subjects were thinking and feeling. Do you see any danger in that? Do you think that the use of this device should be confined to fiction alone?

Lecture Three—Transcript
Narrators—Their Voices and Their Visions

Hello, and welcome to Lecture Three in our course on the "art of reading."

In this lecture, we'll talk about narrators, beginning with the tried and true distinction between first- and third-person narration.

I'm guessing that most of you remember that one from junior high. Still, it probably wouldn't hurt to do a quick refresher. A first-person narrator is an "I" narrator—usually one of the characters—a participant or at least a close observer of the action.

A third-person narrator is a "they," or a "he," or a "she" narrator. This sort of narrator usually remains nameless and may be ageless and sexless as well. Third-person narrators tend to stand outside or above the characters, reporting their actions and moving in and out of their minds. They know all and (eventually) tell all—and that's why they're sometimes called "third-person omniscient, all-knowing, all-seeing narrators."

So far, so good. But so what? That's the real question here—and it's the sort of question that seldom gets asked. Everyone tells you to remember the difference between first- and third-person narrators: your seventh grade English teacher, your eighth grade English teacher, your ninth grade English teacher—they're all over this first- and third-person business, but no one ever tells you why that stuff is worth remembering.

That's what I'd like to do in this lecture. I'll be arguing that there are pros and cons to each kind of narration. There are things you can do with a first-person narrator that you can't do—at least not so easily—with a third-person narrator; and vice versa.

To bolster my case, I'll look at examples from two classic American writers: Edgar Allan Poe and Nathaniel Hawthorne. These authors were born only five years apart—Hawthorne in 1804, and Poe in 1809—and they are tailor-made for comparing and contrasting.

Let's start with Poe. As you probably know, his life story is full of dramatic incidents. He was thrown out of the University of Virginia; he married his 13-year-old cousin; and he was a raging alcoholic—and that's just for starters.

 ©2009 The Teaching Company.

But as I mentioned last time, our concern—in this course, at least—is not with any of those things. That stuff is all about the "man who suffers," right? What we want is the "mind that creates." So our attention must be focused on Poe's writing, on the words he put down for us to read.

All right, then. Poe is most famous for his tales of terror, and almost all of them are told by first-person narrators. If you've read those tales, you'll recall that the narrator is often some kind of madman or maniac. These narrators are not very pleasant, but they do know how to get your attention.

In fact, reading Poe is a little like sitting next to that crazy guy on the bus. You really don't want him to strike up a conversation, but as soon as he does start talking about his cat or the voices in his head, you just can't tear yourself away. You want to know where his story will go and how it will come out.

Let me show you what I mean. These are the opening paragraphs of "The Tell-Tale Heart":

"True!—nervous—very, very dreadfully nervous I had been and am; but why *will* you say that I am mad?"

That's interesting. In the very first sentence, this narrator comes after us. "I'm not crazy," he insists, "just nervous." We've only just met him—and already he's picking a fight with us.

So why is this guy so upset? Why is he so anxious to prove that he's not mad? What difference does it make to him what we think, anyway?

As the narrator moves through the rest of the opening paragraph, he continues to confront us—and to assert his sanity and health. Let me return to the very beginning, so that you can get the full effect:

> True!—nervous—very, very dreadfully nervous I had been and am; but why *will* you say that I am mad? The disease had sharpened my senses—not destroyed—not dulled them. Above all was the sense of hearing acute. I heard all things in the heaven and in the earth. I heard many things in hell. How, then, am I mad? Hearken! and observe how healthily—how calmly I can tell you the whole story.

That's the first paragraph, and in it we sense that this narrator has at least a couple of motives for speaking. The first motive we've already discussed. He wants to convince us that he is sane.

The second motive is a little different. For in addition to insisting that he's not crazy, this narrator also begins to assert his superiority over us. He hears things that we can't hear, remains calm when we might panic. So he suggests that, far from being mad, he's actually a kind of superman—he's more perceptive, more sensitive—certainly more intelligent than the rest of us poor fools.

Already, I think, we can see one of the big advantages of first-person narration: It can make a very powerful first impression. Even if the story starts to drag—which it almost never does in Poe—the reader will probably keep going to the end. Once you've made that initial connection to the storyteller or narrator, it can be almost impossible to break it off.

To clinch this point, I'll ask you to imagine what these paragraphs might be like if Poe had used a third-person narrator. The same information might be conveyed, and some of that same tension might be generated—but the tension probably wouldn't reach the same pitch. Here goes—and remember that this is my version, not Poe's original:

> It was true, he admitted. He had been and still was very, very dreadfully nervous. But he was not mad. The disease had sharpened his senses—not destroyed—not dulled them. And above all his sense of hearing was acute. He heard all things in heaven and earth—and many things in hell, too.

That's my version in the third person, and if I do say so, it's not bad. I could go on that way for quite a while. But even if I held your attention from beginning to end, I could not duplicate the effects that Poe achieves through the use of a first-person narrator.

For example, I'm not sure that I could effectively create the feeling of insanity or madness. I know it would be hard for me to make you feel that you were being confronted or challenged—which is the feeling Poe clearly wants you to get from his version of the passage.

So what happens next in "The Tell-Tale Heart"? If we read on a little further, we'll discover that this narrator is struggling not only with us, but also with himself. He's guilty of a horrible crime—he

 ©2009 The Teaching Company.

murdered an old man—but he still doesn't know why he did it. Here's what he says:

> It is impossible to say how first the idea entered my brain, but once conceived, it haunted me day and night. Object there was none. Passion there was none. I loved the old man. He had never wronged me. He had never given me insult. For his gold I had no desire. I think it was his eye! yes, it was this! He had the eyes of a vulture—a pale blue eye, with a film over it. Whenever it fell upon me, my blood ran cold; and so by degrees—very gradually—I made up my mind to take the life of the old man, and thus rid myself of the eye forever.

In this paragraph, we see that a first-person narrative can become a bit like a monologue or a soliloquy. The narrator may begin by talking to us—but before long, he's talking to himself. He's struggling to understand his own behavior and his own feelings. Poe's narrator doesn't know how he got the idea of murdering the old man—and neither do we.

What's more, we can't resolve the issue by turning to another source of information, because there is no other source—it's just us and this crazy narrator. We have to work with what the narrator gives us. Although that may be more than enough to arouse our curiosity—it's probably not enough to answer our questions.

By now, I'm hoping, you can see that the choice of narrator can make a big difference. First-person narrators tend to capture the reader's attention and imagination. They create a strong sense of immediacy and intimacy—one that's hard to duplicate with third-person narration.

In addition—and this may be even more important—the use of a first-person narrator often forces the reader into a more active role. When you're reading a story that's told in the third person, you're often tempted to sit back. You figure that the narrator knows all and will eventually tell all as I said before. But with a story in the first person, you know you can't make that assumption. You will have to sort through the narrator's motives. You will have to see how reliable or trustworthy he is, and you will have to figure out a few things for yourself.

Finally, I might suggest that first-person narratives almost always raise the question of motivation. Here I'm not thinking of the motivation for murder or any other crime so much as the motivation for storytelling itself. Why do we tell stories in the first place? What are we hoping to accomplish with those stories? Is storytelling an act of confession or is it some sort of rationalization? Can it ever be both at once? Those are the sorts of questions we confront in the best first-person narratives—like "The Tell-Tale Heart."

In wrapping up this part of the lecture, I might note that the tradition of the first-person narrator goes all the way back at least to Chaucer—each of the Canterbury Tales is narrated by a different pilgrim, right? That tradition extends down through Henry James, Joseph Conrad, Ford Madox Ford, and Graham Greene. For a couple of great examples, check out *The Quiet American* by Graham Greene and *The Remains of the Day* by Kazuo Ishiguro.

At this point, it's probably time for us to raise a simple question: If the advantages of first-person narration are so great, then why isn't every story told in the first person? Why do authors ever experiment with other approaches?

Those are good questions, and for the beginnings of an answer we'll turn to some examples from Hawthorne. If Poe is drawn to the first-person narrator for all of the reasons we've been discussing, then Hawthorne is drawn—no less powerfully—to the third-person narrator.

Why? Because Hawthorne actually wants to put some distance between his readers and his characters. Instead of grabbing you by the throat, he keeps you at arm's length. Instead of turning up the heat, he keeps his cool. The last thing he wants is a sense of intimacy or immediacy. Indeed, he seems to delight in throwing his readers off-balance. His narrators like to keep us guessing, and they almost seem to be amused by our confusion.

In making these points, I'm not trying to suggest that such effects are impossible to create in the first person—that's obviously not the case. I'm just saying that if an author wants to create a sense of distance, keep the reader from getting too close to the major characters—third-person narration is probably the way to go.

To develop this claim, I'll turn to one of Hawthorne's most famous tales: "Young Goodman Brown." If you're not familiar with his tales, you really should take a look at them. Truth be told, I prefer Hawthorne's tales to his novels. They have a kind of concentrated power—a strangeness—that is almost unique to American literature.

Our tale, "Young Goodman Brown," is set in Salem, Massachusetts. If that name rings a bell, it should. As Hawthorne knew, Salem was the scene of our nation's most famous witchcraft trials. By setting the scene in Salem, Hawthorne alerts us to the possibility of spooky, supernatural happenings.

At the beginning of the story, a young man named Goodman Brown bids farewell to his lovely, young wife—her name is Faith—and heads off on some sort of journey.

Why is he leaving? Where is he going? Reasonable questions, no doubt—but no answers are ever supplied by Hawthorne's third-person narrator. He simply refuses to let us in on the character's secret.

We are allowed to listen as the young wife asks her husband to reconsider: "Wouldn't it be nicer," she says, "to sleep in your own bed tonight?" We also get a chance to hear Goodman Brown berate himself for leaving.

But at no point in there does the narrator explain the purpose of Goodman Brown's journey. All we're told is that the trip must be completed before sunrise—and that it will take him into the woods outside of town.

Before long, we get the sense that something weird is happening. As Goodman Brown ventures into the dark forest, he meets some very strange characters. One old man carries a staff that looks like a big snake. Indeed, the staff (or snake) almost seems to twist and wiggle as if it were alive.

If that's not bad enough, a bit later Goodman Brown overhears a conversation between this old man and an old woman who complains of losing her broomstick and speaks of being anointed with wolf's bane—and the fat of a newborn baby!

You get the idea. The main point here is that the narrator never identifies the old woman as a witch or the old man as a devil worshipper. He lets us watch and listen, alongside Goodman Brown, as these creepy people get ready for some sort of "communion"—but he steadfastly refuses to explain exactly what they're doing.

That puts us on edge. We're used to seeing third-person narrators as both omniscient and objective, but this narrator is different. He gives us the feeling that he knows more than he's letting on. Indeed, he suggests that he may never tell us everything we want to know.

At this point, it might be interesting to imagine what would happen if Poe were writing this story. Poe would probably use a first-person narrator. That narrator would probably try to convince us that he really did see a couple of people heading off to some weird satanic ritual in the woods. In the end, though we might be engrossed by Poe's version of the story, we wouldn't necessarily believe that narrator. The whole thing would seem interesting, but implausible.

In Hawthorne's version of the story, as I've tried to suggest, we can't escape so quickly. As we read on into the story, we wait and wait for the narrator to announce that it was all some sort of hallucination: Goodman Brown didn't really see an old man with a snake for a staff, and he didn't see any witches, either. It was all a misunderstanding, or a bad dream, or something like that.

As long as the narrator withholds that sort of explanation, he forces us to consider the possibility that it was not a mirage or a figment of Goodman Brown's imagination—that the woods really were full of devil worshippers. So, instead of watching someone else freak out—as we do in a Poe story—we begin to get a little uncomfortable ourselves. Indeed, we begin to want—to need—some more complete account of what really happened out there in the woods.

I don't want to give away the rest of the story—but by now you won't be surprised to learn that Hawthorne's narrator never gives in to our demands. To see what I mean, let's look at the last two paragraphs—the last two paragraphs in the entire story.

Here's the first one: "Had Goodman Brown fallen asleep in the forest, and only dreamed a wild dream of a witch-meeting?"

Here's the beginning of the second paragraph: "Be it so, if you will." So instead of telling us what actually happened, this narrator leaves this up to us to decide—telling us that he doesn't much care either way. If we want it to be a "wild dream," well, that's fine. If we don't, that's OK, too.

How can this narrator be so nonchalant? That's a good question—and the answer emerges in the next few sentences. For in those

 ©2009 The Teaching Company.

sentences we see that the narrator's real concern is not with the reality or unreality of witchcraft in Salem, but rather with the psychological and moral effects of suspicion and doubt: Goodman Brown believes that he's seen something truly horrible—and so, it might as well be true.

If it was a dream, the narrator explains, "it was a dream of evil omen for young Goodman Brown. A stern, a sad, a darkly meditative, a distrustful, if not a desperate, man did he become from the night of that fearful dream."

With that sentence, the narrator swings us into his conclusion and begins to sum up the rest of Brown's life. As I read the rest of the paragraph, listen for a subtle shift in tone—because at this point, the narrator is no longer being playful, no longer being evasive. Now he tells us exactly what happened—in no uncertain terms.

> On the Sabbath day [the narrator explains] when the congregation were singing a holy psalm, he [that is, Young Goodman Brown] could not listen, because an anthem of sin rushed loudly upon his ear and drowned all the blessed strain. When the minister spoke from the pulpit, with power and fervid eloquence, and with his hand on the open Bible, of the sacred truths of our religion, and of saint-like lives and triumphant deaths, and of future bliss or misery unutterable, then did Goodman Brown turn pale, dreading lest the roof should thunder down upon the grey blasphemer and his hearers. Often, awaking suddenly at midnight, he shrank from the bosom of Faith; and at morning or eventide, when the family knelt down to prayer, he scowled, and muttered to himself, and gazed sternly at his wife, and turned away. And when he had lived long, and was borne to his grave, a hoary corpse, followed by Faith, an aged woman, and children and grandchildren, a goodly procession, besides neighbors not a few, they carved no hopeful verse upon his tombstone; for his dying hour was gloom.

Got that? "[H]is dying hour was gloom." There's no room for doubt there. This is what happens when you're crippled by a sense of sinfulness: You pull away from your wife and your neighbors. You always expect to be crushed or destroyed—after all, that's what you think you deserve.

How much of that could have been conveyed by a first-person narrator? If Brown himself were the narrator—and, really, he's the only logical choice—he might tell the story from his deathbed. He might explain what happened in the woods and then talk about his later distrust for his wife. In short, he might look back on a long life and see no hope for redemption or release.

But isn't that about all he could do? How, for example, could he take us up to his own dying hour? Oh, sure, he might say: "My own dying hour will be gloom." But that's just not as final; it's not as definitive—at least not to my ears—as the ending that we get from Hawthorne's third-person narrator.

So, maybe now we're ready to admit that there are some distinct advantages to third-person narration. With a third-person narrator, there may, indeed, be a loss of immediacy and intensity. You may not get that same sense of almost overwhelming closeness—but maybe that's OK.

Maybe there are times, as a matter of fact, when a writer might want to distance us from his characters. Maybe there are other times when the writer would like to provide some information or insight that's unavailable to the characters themselves. At such times, third-person narration definitely has its advantages.

In case you're worried, this sort of narration doesn't have to be flat and lifeless. After all, Hawthorne's narrator has lots of personality. Indeed, he is highly intelligent and supremely playful. He knows what we expect from third-person narration, and he makes a game of his unwillingness to play along.

So, yes, it matters what kind of narrator is used. Just think what would be lost if Poe tried to write like Hawthorne—or Hawthorne like Poe—and you'll see what a big difference it can make.

Is that it, then? Does it have to be an either-or decision? Is there any way to split the difference between first- and third-person narration—any way to enjoy the advantages of both forms at the very same time?

Yes—as a matter of fact, there is. If you master one very simple trick, you can enjoy some of the immediacy and intimacy associated with first-person narration while remaining in the third person. Here's how it works. Your third-person narrator begins to borrow

©2009 The Teaching Company.

little bits of language—a word or two, maybe a whole phrase—from one or more of the characters.

Those words don't have to be set off in quotation marks or identified with some sort of "tag." In fact, it's better if they're left unmarked—because marking and tagging tends to slow things down. It interferes with our experience of the story.

There is a name for this trick or device. It's called "free indirect discourse" or "free indirect style," and according to most critics, it is the thing that makes modern fiction—well, modern. If you've never heard of it before, don't worry. This is not the sort of thing they teach you in junior high.

Free indirect discourse is associated with authors from Jane Austen to James Joyce and beyond. But it's most closely linked to Gustave Flaubert, the author of *Madame Bovary* and *A Sentimental Education*—and so, we'll turn to him for an example.

Our example comes from the middle of *Madame Bovary*. Emma Bovary has just begun an adulterous affair—and she couldn't be more delighted. Indeed, the author says that it's as if "a second puberty had come to her"—as if she were "entering upon marvels where all would be passion, ecstasy, delirium."

If that sounds overblown—maybe even a little nuts—that's because it's supposed to. Much of this language is coming not from the narrator, but rather from Emma herself.

She's read a million trashy novels, and now she's starting to imagine her own story in the very same way: as a passionate romance, with herself as the heroine.

Are you with me so far? OK. As I read on, be on the lookout for more of this overblown language. Here goes:

> An azure infinity encompassed her, the heights of sentiment sparkled under her thought, and ordinary existence appeared only afar off, down below in the shade, through the interspaces of these heights. … Had she not suffered enough? But now she triumphed, and the love so long pent up burst forth in full joyous bubblings. She tasted it without remorse, without anxiety, without trouble.

See how that works? We're still in the third person, but we're getting some of the feel and flavor of first-person narration. Free indirect discourse allows us to be both inside and outside the character at the very same time.

This is not the oldest trick in the book—most theorists see it emerging in the early decades of the 19th century—but, as I say, it's one of the best and one of the most important, too.

So does that exhaust our options? Is there anything besides first person, third person, and free indirect discourse? Of course, there is—though these other possibilities aren't nearly as common.

It is possible, for example, to shift between first- and third-person narrators—as Dickens does in *Bleak House*. It's also possible to shift among several first-person narrators, as Faulkner does in *The Sound and the Fury* or *As I Lay Dying*. It's also possible, I think, to create a kind of "we" narrator, a second-person narrator, and that's what Jeffrey Eugenides does in *The Virgin Suicides*; that's what Joshua Ferris does in his recent novel, *Then We Came to the End*.

Finally, you can write in the second person, and that's what one of my favorites, Lorrie Moore, does in some of her early short stories. Here's a quick example taken from a story called "How to Become a Writer":

> Write another story about a man and a woman who, in the very first paragraph, have their lower torsos accidentally blitzed away by dynamite. In the second paragraph, with the insurance money, they buy a frozen yogurt stand together. There are six more paragraphs. You read the whole thing out loud in class. No one likes it. They say your sense of plot is outrageous and incompetent. After class someone asks you if you are crazy.

I don't know if it would be possible to sustain that effect over the course of an entire novel, but Moore works wonders with it in these early stories. (She's just a terrific writer.)

OK, I think that that brings us to a nice stopping point. So right here, I'd like to review some of the main points that we've made in this lecture and point ahead to the next one. First, we've kind of refined our sense of the difference between first-person and third-person narration, and we've also gotten some idea of why that distinction matters—what you can do with one sort of narrator that you can't do with another. Maybe—just maybe—we're beginning to realize that the choice of a narrator is crucial to the larger effect of a story. I would suggest that the next time you're 9 or 10 pages into a new book, maybe at the end of the first section or chapter, you just ask yourself a few simple questions: Is this in first person or third person? How would it be different if it were the other way around? That second question is a little harder, but before long you'll get the hang of it. In the end, it's not a simple matter of classifying or categorizing the narrator, but rather a more challenging and rewarding task. What happens as a result of this particular choice, what possibilities are created, what effects are achieved—when you commit to one sort of narrator instead of another? We'll return to these questions throughout the rest of the course. In our next lecture, however, we'll turn from authors and narrators to characters—taking our example from the work of the Russian short story master, Anton Chekhov. Thanks as always for joining us. We'll look forward to seeing you again soon.

Lecture Four
Characters—Beyond Round and Flat

Scope:

For many readers, nothing is more important than the characters. Do we like these people? Can we root for them or relate to them? Are they good role models? If the answers to those questions are in any way disappointing, many readers will conclude that the entire work is boring or pointless. The aim of this lecture will be to develop a wider and more intelligent range of responses to literary characters. For the artful reader, we will discover, the real question is not whether the characters are likable; it is whether they embody a sensitive, intelligent understanding of human motivation, memory, and desire.

Outline

I. In this lecture, we explore a subject of undeniable importance and nearly endless fascination: characters.

    A. For many readers, nothing is more important than the characters.

    B. The problem is compounded by the fact that many of our greatest writers hardly ever write about nice people. Look, for instance, at Fyodor Dostoevsky or Philip Roth.

    C. I hope to enlarge your sense of what makes a character interesting or worth reading about.

II. Here are some questions and caveats that we will consider.

    A. Questions: How far should we go with this niceness thing? What makes a character interesting?

    B. Caveats.

        1. We will be talking about the lead character.

        2. We will be talking about literary fiction.

        3. There are different rules and different expectations for different kinds of books.

        4. We are dealing with characters from the last 200 years or so; novelistic characters are essentially different from the figures we usually find in Homer or Shakespeare.

 ©2009 The Teaching Company.

III. We look at an example from Anton Chekhov, the great Russian short story writer.

    A. Chekhov is admired most especially for his characters. He has a reputation for treating his characters generously, and he tries to encourage the same sort of generosity in his readers.

    B. A perfect example is a story called "The Lady with the Dog," in which our development as readers subtly parallels the development of the characters themselves.

    C. What can we take away from this example?

        1. A character does not have to be likable or admirable to be interesting.

        2. An unlikable character can change and grow.

        3. Change and growth do not necessarily ensure a character's happiness.

        4. We should get in the habit of monitoring our responses to characters.

IV. We move on to some broader generalizations about characters and characterization.

    A. Round characters, which are dynamic, complex, and unpredictable, are more interesting than flat ones.

    B. This distinction comes to us from E. M. Forster's book *Aspects of the Novel*. After introducing the distinction between flat and round characters, Forster says, "The test of a round character is whether it is capable of surprising in a convincing way."

V. Can we go beyond roundness and flatness and extend our thinking about characters and characterization? Yes, there are certain qualities or attributes common to many interesting fictional characters.

    A. There is some sort of internal conflict or struggle.

    B. There has to be a crisis. The crisis often includes some sort of reckoning with the past and may also require a reckoning with the self.

Suggested Reading:

Forster, *Aspects of the Novel*, chap. 4.

Scholes, Phelan, and Kellogg, *The Nature of Narrative*, chap. 5.

Questions to Consider:

1. Do you ever find yourself drawn to flawed or even unsavory characters? Are there some sorts of characters you simply would rather not read about—no matter how well the story is told?

2. Can you apply Forster's theory of characterization to the real world? Is your family or your office full of round characters? Do you think you know any flat characters—people whose behavior often strikes you as predictable or typical?

©2009 The Teaching Company.

Lecture Four—Transcript
Characters—Beyond Round and Flat

Hello, and welcome to Lecture Four in our course on the "art of reading."

In this lecture, we'll move on to a subject of undeniable importance and nearly endless fascination: the characters. For many readers, nothing is more important than the characters.

Oh, they're interested in the author, and the implied author, and the narrator. But for these readers, the characters are the single most important element of the work. If the characters are interesting and likable—if we can root for them or relate to them—then the work is a success. If, on the other hand, the characters are boring or unlikable, if they do things that we don't understand or can't accept—well, then the work is a failure.

This attitude is not entirely unreasonable. In many ways, it makes perfect sense. When you pick up a novel, you're making a big commitment. It's not like sitting down for another rerun on TV. You may be working on the book for several days—maybe several weeks, if you're busy with other things—and you don't want to spend that time fighting against the characters. If they're unpleasant, or immoral, or worse, why not put the book down and find something else to read?

As I say, this is not a bad question, and the problem is compounded by the fact that many of our greatest writers hardly ever write about nice people. Look, for instance, at Dostoevsky—or, if you prefer a more recent example, Philip Roth. Their characters are needy, selfish, and dishonest. They do all kinds of bad things, and they also have very, very bad habits: drinking, sexual infidelity, meanness—and that's just for starters. So we might well ask: Why? Why should we have to read about these people?

The purpose of this lecture is to address those questions in a serious way. By the end of the lecture, I may not have convinced you to run out and get *Crime and Punishment*—or even *Portnoy's Complaint*. But I hope I will have enlarged your sense of what makes a character "interesting" or "worth reading about."

A quick overview of the upcoming lecture, then. We'll start with a few questions and some caveats—kind of like stretching before a run or a workout. Then we'll turn to an example from Anton Chekhov. Why Chekhov? For many reasons, really—not the least of which is that his approach to characterization has been a major influence on later writers.

After looking at Chekhov, we'll consider some broader generalizations about characters and characterization. Among these will be the familiar distinction, first devised by E. M. Forster, between "flat" characters and "round" ones. This distinction remains useful—it will help us to see what's going on in Chekhov—but it doesn't exhaust the subject of characterization, and so we'll need to look for ways of moving beyond it.

OK, then. Questions.

Number one: How far should we go with this whole "niceness" thing? If it's possible for a character to be too nasty, is it also possible for a character to be too nice? Look at it this way: What kind of story can you tell about a really, really nice person?

I suppose you can always show nice people triumphing over adversity. A nice guy gets dumped by his wife. He meets an attractive young widow and takes a second chance on love. Or, a nice lady gets fired by her piggish boss—"Oh, I hate him!"—and starts over again as a caterer, or a winemaker, or a dog trainer.

There are lots of stories like that, and I suppose they're not all bad. They're never very surprising, though. You'll always know how they're going to come out. The nice guy will start out being surrounded by meanies and creeps—but in the end niceness will prevail. It may take a while. There may be twists and turns along the way—but niceness will prevail.

Maybe it's the predictability of these stories that makes them so popular. I don't know for sure. For now, I'm just wondering if we shouldn't revisit the expectation that characters must be likable or admirable. Mixed in with the niceness, I suspect, we also need to find some—well, not-so-niceness.

Question number two: If niceness is not the be-all and end-all, then what should we be looking for instead? What does make a character interesting? What kind of character tends to make you want to go on reading?

 ©2009 The Teaching Company.

Questions about niceness, then, and questions about alternatives to niceness. We're trying, in short, to find out what separates a great character—a really interesting or compelling character—from characters that seem lifeless, or drab, or predictable.

Now for a few quick caveats.

First, as we move ahead, we'll be talking about the lead character, not the members of the supporting cast.

Second, we'll be talking about literary fiction—as opposed to what we might loosely call "pulp fiction." By "pulp fiction," I simply mean the sort of thing you might find on sale at the drugstore or the airport: westerns, legal thrillers, spy stories, sci-fi—that kind of thing.

That last point comes from my wife—a librarian and devoted reader who likes to remind me that there are different rules for different kinds of books. What works for the hero of a western won't necessarily work for the hero of a mystery story.

My wife adds another observation. She says that some of the best popular writers take a form that's not essentially character-driven and try to give the characters a little more depth or shading. Her example here is P. D. James, the great British mystery writer.

One final caveat. We're dealing with characters from the last 200 years or so—if you like, from Jane Austen on down to the present. Here, I'm not following my nearest and dearest—but rather scholars like Robert Scholes and Robert Kellogg, who suggest that "novelistic characters" are essentially different from the figures we usually find in Homer or even in Shakespeare.

What is the difference? According to Scholes and Kellogg, it has a lot to do with increasing attention to "aspirations, suppressed desires" and with the shift to what they call a "psychological presentation of the inner life."

I don't know enough about earlier forms of narrative to take the argument much further.

(My specialty is the development of the modern novel.) Still, I might observe that Shakespeare seldom provides the sort of detail we expect from a writer like Jane Austen. He never tells us how many children were born to Lady Macbeth, for example—and in the end it doesn't really matter to him. Shakespeare can tell his stories without getting into any of those details.

My point here is not really all that tricky. In this lecture and throughout the entire course, we're dealing with particular sorts of characters and particular approaches to characterization. So we can't assume that our conclusions will apply across the board. Indeed, they probably won't apply to westerns, or horror stories, or fantasy novels—or even to Shakespeare plays.

Fair enough. Now that we're done with questions and caveats, we can move on to an example from Chekhov, the great Russian short story writer. Chekhov was born in 1860, and he died in 1904. He was actually the master of two different forms—for in addition to writing hundreds of short stories, he also wrote for the theatre. His best-known plays are *The Seagull*, *The Three Sisters*, *Uncle Vanya*, and *The Cherry Orchard*.

His influence on later fiction writers—well, it can only be described as massive. (If you want to compliment a writer, just tell her that her stuff is "Chekhovian.") As I suggested before, Chekhov is admired most especially for his characters. He has a reputation for treating the characters generously, for resisting cheap shots and snap judgments.

As we'll see, he tries to encourage the same sort of generosity in his readers. He doesn't simply want to portray the experience of emotional growth or development—he wants to inspire it as well.

To show you what I mean, I'll turn to a story called "The Lady with the Dog." This is now a kind of signature piece for Chekhov. It's widely anthologized and widely admired. (Indeed, it's been described as "the all-time short story gold standard.") In case you're wondering, we'll be using the translation by Constance Garnett, since it's available almost everywhere.

The main character in "The Lady with the Dog" is Dmitri Dmitrich Gurov. He's on holiday in Yalta, a Russian resort town, and he's heard rumors about the arrival of yet another tourist: a lady with a little dog.

We learn that he's interested in meeting her—and then we learn more. Gurov is in his late thirties—pushing 40, really—with a daughter and two sons. If he was ever in love with his wife, that feeling is long gone. He now thinks that she's boring, narrow-

©2009 The Teaching Company.

minded, and inelegant. At the same time, he also thinks that she's a little frightening. The bottom line is that he just doesn't like to spend much time at home.

But even that's not all. For as the narrator explains: "He had begun being unfaithful to her long ago—had been unfaithful to her often, and, probably on that account, almost always spoke ill of women, and when they were talked about in his presence, used to call them 'the lower race.'"

Great. This guy cheats on his wife, and he makes insulting remarks about women. So if he dislikes women so much, why does he keep on having these affairs? Actually, he doesn't really know. He realizes that his affairs almost always lead to trouble, but—and here again, I'm quoting—"at every fresh meeting with an interesting woman, this experience [of the earlier affairs] seemed to slip out of his memory, and he was eager for life, and everything seemed simple and amusing."

So, our initial impressions of Gurov—they're not favorable. He's not evil—but he sure is shallow, and his treatment of women leaves much to be desired. Still, there's no denying that he's interesting. He can't seem to control himself, and so he seems likely to end up in trouble again.

You can't help but wonder what he'll do next. Will he stop playing around with other women? Seems unlikely, but at this point anything is possible. If he doesn't stop playing around, then what will make his next affair different from all the rest?

Maybe this time, the tables will be turned. You get the feeling that he's usually the one to break things off—so maybe this time, he'll get dumped. That would be interesting, wouldn't it?

These are great questions—the sort of questions that you find yourself asking about a really interesting character. If I were you, I'd get in the habit of asking such questions, and I'd make a point of asking them deliberately. I'd take a moment to sketch two or three possibilities: Gurov stops playing around; he gets dumped—and see how each of them looks to you.

Which scenarios seem most likely? Which would be the most satisfying to you as a reader? Which would make you laugh? Which would make you cry? If you have these possibilities in mind as you read ahead, you'll almost certainly feel more closely, more tightly, connected to the characters and more deeply involved in their stories.

Enough for now—let's get back to Chekhov. As it turns out, Gurov does not stop playing around. In fact, it doesn't take long before he moves in on the lady with the dog. (Her name, we learn, is Anna.) A week passes, and sure enough they become lovers. Some more time passes, and Anna gets a letter from her husband—that's right, she's married too—and so she returns home.

At this point, Gurov is not especially upset. Indeed, he seems ready to move on, which probably means move on to another affair. So he returns to Moscow, where he tries to resume his normal life—but he finds that this time, he just can't do it. A month passes, and his memory of the affair has only grown more vivid.

So what does he do? Something he's never done before. He tells his wife he's going away on business and heads straight for the town where Anna lives with her husband. As I say, he's never done anything like this before—and doesn't know why he's doing it now. He's improvising. He's making it all up as he goes along.

When he gets to Anna's town, he stakes out her house. He waits outside for her to appear, but that doesn't work, and he's about ready to give up—when he decides to take one more chance, because he's got a hunch that he might run into her at the theatre. So off he goes to the premiere of a play called *The Geisha*.

Before I finish this story, let me ask you to look at how reckless he's being. Look at how much he's risking! He doesn't know how Anna will react—he hasn't told her that he's coming—and yet there he is, roaming around her hometown, basically stalking her.

So, old Gurov turns out to be a very interesting character indeed. There's much more to him than we might ever have expected. Who knows? He may even prove himself capable of love.

If you really don't want me to spoil the story, you need to stop now. Just hit the pause button and start us up again when you're done reading. Still there? OK, then. Here goes.

It turns out Anna is in agony. She has thought of nothing but Gurov—and she can't believe that he's shown up at the theatre. She's mortified. People are watching, but he kisses her anyway—and

©2009 The Teaching Company.

that's it. From that point on, they are back together. She says that she'll come to visit him in Moscow, and so she does.

They get in the habit of meeting in hotel rooms—and as the story closes, we see how Gurov has been transformed by their relationship. He feels compassion and tenderness for Anna, and the narrator explains that the two of them "forgave each other for what they were ashamed of in their past, they forgave everything in the present, and felt that this love of theirs had changed them both."

So, the story has a happy ending? Not exactly—as novelist Charles Baxter points out, this love almost "feels like a punishment."

Why is that? Gurov is left with no idea of what to do. He has Anna, but he doesn't have anything else. As the story ends, he and Anna are committed to one another—but they also realize that they have "a long, long road before them." What's more, the narrator tells us— and this is the very last line in the story—"the most complicated and difficult part of it was only just beginning."

So, as Baxter says, Gurov gets what he wants—and finds that there's no way for him to enjoy it.

The great thing about all of this—the thing that makes this story such a perfect example—is that our development as readers subtly parallels the development of the characters themselves. Gurov begins by thinking of Anna as yet another conquest, and he ends up feeling great compassion for her. So, too, do we move from thinking of Gurov as a self-centered jerk to viewing him as a man capable of deep feeling and genuine sympathy.

What can we take away from this example? What larger conclusions might we draw from our encounter with Chekhov? Several, I think.

First, a character does not have to be likable or admirable to be interesting. It may be, in fact, that flawed characters have more potential.

Second, an unlikable character can change and grow. We may not like the character we meet at the beginning, but we shouldn't assume that he'll still be around at the end.

Third, change and growth—though positive experiences—don't necessarily ensure a character's happiness. We may have to see growth not as a means to an end, but rather as an end in itself.

Finally, we should get in the habit of monitoring our responses to the characters. I've mentioned this before, I know, but it's worth repeating. What are our first impressions? Do our feelings ever change—and if so, what might account for that development? When and how does the story ask us to reconsider our views?

With those questions in mind, we might move on to some broader generalizations about characters and characterization. Here, as before, we'll be looking to see what makes some characters more interesting, more compelling and more memorable, than others.

Let's begin with a familiar notion: that "round" characters are more interesting than "flat" ones. I'm guessing you've heard this one before. Round characters are dynamic, complex, and unpredictable. Flat characters are just the opposite. They don't change. Whenever they appear, we know exactly what they're going to do and exactly what they're going to say.

This familiar distinction actually comes to us from E. M. Forster, the author of novels like *Howards End* and *A Passage to India*. In 1927, Forster collected a number of his lectures into a book called *Aspects of the Novel*. This book is still in print—and it should be, because it makes some very subtle points in a very entertaining way.

After introducing the distinction between flat and round characters, Forster poses a brilliant question: How can you tell if a character is round or flat? What kind of test can you run for that?

As you might imagine, he had a good answer up his sleeve. Here's what he said:

> The test of a round character is whether it is capable of surprising in a convincing way. If it never surprises, it is flat. If it does not convince, it is a flat pretending to be round. It must have the incalculability of life about it—life within the pages of a book.

Before moving on, let's take that statement apart. We know what Forster means by "surprising"—but what about "convincing"? That's the tricky part.

To work through this problem, we'll need to consider a few hypothetical examples. So let's go back to Chekhov and ask ourselves how we'd feel if Gurov ended the story by breaking off with Anna and returning to his wife. He parts from Anna, he goes

©2009 The Teaching Company.

back home, and suddenly realizes that what he's really wanted—all along—is a passionate connection to his wife.

That would be surprising, but not convincing. Everything we know about Gurov's wife makes it seem unbelievable. For one thing, she's nothing like Anna. For another thing, she finds Gurov ridiculous—so what could he possibly get out of a renewed relationship with her? So, no—if he went back to his wife, we'd have an unconvincing surprise, and Gurov and Chekhov would both fail the E. M. Forster roundness test.

How, then, does Gurov manage to pass? What makes the actual surprise—his unexpected devotion to Anna—seem convincing in the end? I think it has something to do with his complex, contradictory attitude toward women.

If you look back at the opening of the story, you'll see that although he refers to women as the "lower race," Gurov prefers the company of women to that of men. Women make him feel "free." They put him "at ease with himself." It may be, then, that he's grown tired of playing around and is ready to fall in love with someone who might actually return his affection—someone, in other words, like Anna.

That would be my guess, anyway. Gurov is interesting, his story moving and compelling, because he's a round character. He surprises in a convincing way.

Is that all there is to it? Can we go beyond roundness and flatness and extend our thinking about characters and characterization? I think so. In fact, I would submit that there are lots of other things for us to be on the lookout for. Here, then, is a brief list of qualities or attributes common to many—if not all—interesting fictional characters. (In making this list, I must add, I'm once again indebted to Charles Baxter, whose writings on the subject of characterization are right up there with Forster's.)

OK, then. First item on our list: some sort of internal conflict or struggle. The operative word here is "internal." Interesting characters may or may not be in conflict with other characters, but they are almost always in conflict with themselves.

Such conflicts can take several forms. The most basic—and the most familiar—is probably the struggle between good and evil, the wish to be virtuous and the temptation to sin. This sort of conflict is not all that hard to portray as fans of Bugs Bunny or Homer Simpson can attest. You just put an angel on one shoulder and a devil on the other, and you're all set.

A little juicier, a little richer—at least in my opinion—is the conflict between desire and fear: You want to talk to that girl (or guy), but you're afraid of being rejected. Even more interesting are conflicts between competing desires: You want to find a home or a family, but you also want to be independent and self-sufficient. Why is that more interesting? In that case, it's not really clear what you ought to do. The conflict seems less like make-believe and a little more like real life.

It's possible to make things even more interesting. This time, let's say that there's a conflict between what you want and what you want to want. What you want and what you want to want. So how would that work? Let's say that you are a skinny, rather dimwitted guy—and you're stranded on a desert island. (Let's say, in other words, that you are the title character from the old TV classic, *Gilligan's Island*.)

Let's say, completing the scenario, that the island is also home to a beautiful movie star (Ginger) and a wholesome girl-next-door type (Mary Ann)—and you want Ginger. You have it really, really bad for her. But you know that Ginger has no interest in you: She wouldn't go for you if you were the last man on earth—and really, living on that desert island and all, you pretty much are.

All of that is clear to you, and so is this: Your problems would be solved if you could only convince yourself to want Mary Ann. She's nice, she's pretty, and she seems to spend a lot of time hanging around your hut. So just do it! Just go ahead: Fall in love with Mary Ann—not Ginger—Mary Ann.

See how that works? I know it's a silly example, but it helps to clarify the point. You can't always control your own desires. You don't always want what you want to want. When that sort of conflict arises your story is likely to be a good one.

OK, let's move on. In addition to internal conflict, there has to be a crisis, some event that brings the conflict out into the open. Your aging father tells you that he's fallen in love with a nurse at the assisted living facility. Your son gets kicked out of school—and his principal turns out to be Ginger.

See how that works? The conflict has been there all along, but it was buried or submerged. There was no particular reason to deal with it. But now, because of the crisis, you simply have no choice. Your father's thing with this nurse forces you to admit that you've always hated the way he treated your mother. You've always blamed him for their divorce, and you don't really see why he deserves any sort of love from anyone.

Now we're talking, right? This really could get interesting—and this, I believe, is just the sort of character and the sort of story you should be looking for: a real conflict, not a phony one; a real crisis, with no easy answers in sight.

Are there other qualities we might add to our list—other things that we can say about this sort of conflict or crisis?

Yes. First, the crisis often includes some sort of reckoning with the past. The character is forced to question his own motives or reflect on his own desires. So, why do I blame my father for the divorce? Why should I resent his happiness? This crisis may also require a reckoning with the self—or, more specifically, with a cherished image of the self.

Let's say that you tend to think of yourself as a generous person—a kind and forgiving person—and let's say that lots of other people seem to agree with you. They seem in lots of different ways to trust and respect you.

Now here you are, looking for reasons to dislike your father's new girlfriend. She's a nurse, for crying out loud! She's the one who's really kind and generous—not you! So how did you get to be such a creep? Have you always been this way? How do you know that you haven't been hiding your true feelings—and your true self—for all these years? How do you know that this isn't your day of reckoning—the day when you're forced to admit that you are a jerk?

We started with a simple question: What makes a character interesting or worth reading about?—and we've worked our way to what seems like a pretty good answer. To review, then: An interesting character passes the test for roundness. He or she is capable of surprising in a convincing way. An interesting character has to deal with some sort of internal conflict. It may be a conflict between sin and virtue, or between desires and fears. It may even be a conflict between competing desires: what you want and what you want to want. An interesting character is also forced to deal with a crisis—an event or experience that forces the central conflict out of its hiding places. There may also be a reckoning with the past, with the self, or—and this is really my favorite—with some sort of self-image. By the way, isn't that what happens to Gurov, the character in the Chekhov story? He cherishes an image of himself as a happy-go-lucky ladies' man, but he discovers that he's actually a person of great depth and feeling—a true romantic, instead.

With all of that on the table, you can probably see why this sort of thing seldom happens in a mystery, or a western, or a legal thriller. In those stories, it would just get in the way of solving the crime or running the bad guys out of town.

In what—for lack of a better term—I'm calling "literary fiction," this sort of thing is the whole point of the story. We read about these characters to know how they'll surprise us—to see if and when they'll settle their conflict, how they'll revise their understandings of the past and of themselves.

That seems like a good place for us to stop. In our next lecture, we'll consider another crucial element of fiction—description—asking how descriptions of characters and settings can contribute to our experience of a work.

Thanks as always for joining us. We'll look forward to seeing you soon.

 ©2009 The Teaching Company.

Lecture Five
Descriptions—People, Places, and Things

Scope:

If you are the kind of reader who usually skips over descriptions, you do not need to feel guilty. Long descriptions may be full of meaningful symbols and beautiful phrases, but at times they seem to go on forever. What are descriptions meant to do for the reader? Why should we think twice before skipping over them? In pursuing such questions, we will consider two classic short stories from the middle of the 20th century: "Pigeon Feathers," by John Updike, and "Revelation," by Flannery O'Connor. For both Updike and O'Connor, as for many other writers, description not only sets the stage for later events; it trains our senses and awakens our spirits. To look closely and describe carefully may indeed be an act of devotion, a source of deeper understanding and genuine self-knowledge.

Outline

I. In this lecture, our aim will be to find an alternative to skipping descriptions. We will see that a good description not only creates a vivid impression; it also raises questions and opens up new possibilities.

II. We start with Updike's "Pigeon Feathers."

    A. The central character in "Pigeon Feathers" is David Kern, whose family has just moved from a small town to the farm where his mother was raised.

    B. He is not happy about the move, and the opening descriptions help us to see why. The first thing to be described in detail is a book: a volume from *The Outline of History*, by H. G. Wells. The description helps to convey David's feelings toward his parents—and toward all adults.

    C. A good description not only helps to set the scene or create a vivid impression. It also serves a larger purpose, helping us to understand how the world looks and feels to the characters.

    D. You cannot always deal with descriptions separately. You also need to look for patterns or connections. The descriptions of the father and grandmother work to reinforce the earlier association of the book with the ugly, decaying adult world.

E. David's crisis is a spiritual crisis. The resolution is conveyed largely through detailed descriptions. In this case, the descriptions focus on the bodies of animals: the family dog and then pigeons.

F. Is everything in the story described in such great detail? Interestingly, no. In addition to noticing what is described, you should also notice what is not described. Whether a description is omitted on purpose or by accident, its absence can be very revealing.

III. In Flannery O'Connor's work, detailed description of people, places, and things is always an essential part of the drama. We turn to a story called "Revelation."

A. The initial setting for this story is the waiting room of a doctor's office. The room is described in some detail, but most of our attention is focused on the people.
 1. Introduced first are the Turpins—Claud and his wife.
 2. Mrs. Turpin is a major character—indeed, everyone and everything else in the waiting room is described through her "bright black eyes," narrated through free indirect discourse.

B. What general conclusions can we draw from O'Connor's initial descriptions?
 1. Like Updike, she seems to understand that it is more interesting to show things from a particular point of view.
 2. As the first part of the story unfolds, we are introduced to nine other characters—each of them is seen and judged by Mrs. Turpin.

C. These examples show us that in some cases, descriptions do not simply add to the story—they tell the story. In a sense, they are the story.

D. O'Connor was never afraid to acknowledge that detailed descriptions were vitally important to her work.

E. But what is the controlling purpose in this particular story?
 1. First she wants us to see what Mrs. Turpin is like.
 2. Then she wants to trick us into behaving like Mrs. Turpin to convince us that the story is something more than a satirical look at a fat, foolish lady.

F. As in the case of the Updike story, there is something that is not described.

    1. We do not hear what the people are wearing.

    2. That is because it no longer matters and has never mattered.

    3. This is Mrs. Turpin's revelation.

    4. And now she has a chance—and a choice.

G. For both Updike and O'Connor, observation and description have a spiritual dimension.

IV. A review.

  A. It is OK to skip descriptions when they seem formulaic or slow down the action.

  B. But skipping is not OK, or at least not advisable, in most other cases.

    1. In those cases, details are not merely presented.

    2. Most often, they are presented from a particular point of view.

    3. They help us to see what the characters see, and so they may also lead us to rethink our place in the story.

  C. In conclusion, sometimes things that seem trivial or cosmetic or even ornamental—like passages of description— are directly connected to the largest, most urgent issues in fiction.

Suggested Reading:

O'Connor, "The Nature and Aim of Fiction."

———, "Writing Short Stories."

Updike, "Why Write?"

Questions to Consider:

1. How much description is too much? How much is too little? Could you do without physical descriptions of the major characters, for example? Or do you find that they are somehow crucial to your reading experience?

2. "It is a good deal easier for most people to state an abstract idea than to describe and thus re-create some object that they actually see." Or so said Flannery O'Connor. Do you agree? Would you find it easier to expound upon the beauties of nature or describe the scene outside your window?

Lecture Five—Transcript
Descriptions—People, Places, and Things

Hello, and welcome to Lecture Five in our course on the "art of reading."

Our first few lectures treated the reader's relationships to authors, implied authors, narrators, and characters. In this lecture, we'll talk about descriptions—detailed accounts of people, places, and things.

Let me begin by offering a few words of comfort. If you're the kind of reader who usually skips over descriptions, you need not despair—for you're not alone. In some works, especially older works, descriptions can seem to go on forever. It's as if the narrator hits the "pause button," stopping the action to tell us about every single tree in the forest.

I love old books, but even I have to admit to some frustration with an author like Sir Walter Scott. We'll be talking about Scott in one of our upcoming lectures, but for now it may be enough to say that the narrator of *Ivanhoe* does, indeed, stop to describe each of the major characters from head to toe.

If you compare the descriptions of the book's two heroines, Rowena and Rebecca, you can see that they are highly formulaic. We start with a quick appraisal of the character's form and figure. Then it's on to the face: complexion, eyes and eyebrows—and, of course, the hair. Finally, we end with jewelry and clothing. There are a few more details in the case of Rebecca—but the basic approach to describing both characters is exactly the same.

Even I couldn't fault you for skipping over that sort of thing. If you want to know the truth, I sometimes do it myself.

Still, it's worth noting that some classic authors handle descriptions in a much different way. Jane Austen was writing at exactly the same time as Scott—and she never, ever hits the pause button or overwhelms the reader with detail.

With this qualification in place, I'm ready to give you a quick overview of the upcoming lecture. Our aim will be to find an alternative to skipping descriptions. In pursuit of that goal, we'll consider the work of two writers: John Updike and Flannery O'Connor. As we consider their uses of description, we'll see that a good description not only creates a vivid impression—it also raises questions and opens up new possibilities.

As it turns out, then, description is not a separate topic. It's closely related to all of our other topics—and handled expertly, it can deepen our understanding of the characters and sharpen our interest in the story.

Let's start with Updike—and, more specifically, with "Pigeon Feathers," one of his most important early stories. It's sometimes said to be the story in which he really found his voice—and when he died in the winter of 2009, the story was quoted in *The New York Times* and *The New Yorker* magazine.

The central character in "Pigeon Feathers" is David Kern, a boy of 14, whose family has just moved from a small town to the farm where his mother was raised. He's not happy about the move, and the opening descriptions of the crowded, dingy farmhouse help us to see why.

The first things to be described are things—objects, pieces of furniture—and the first of them to be described in detail is a book: a volume from *The Outline of History* by H. G. Wells.

The description of the book goes on for the better part of a page. By the time it's over, we've encountered lots of specific details: the faded color of the binding; the book's nasty, "sweetish" smell; the look of his mother's signature on the flyleaf; the size and shape of the print; and the yellow edges of the pages themselves.

Why spend so much time on these details? The most obvious answer is that they help to make the book seem real, giving us a clear sense of how this thing would feel if we could hold it in our hands.

There's more to it than that, however. After all, any set of details would make the book seem real. So, why these details? Why should the book be old instead of new? Why should it belong to his mother instead of his father? Why couldn't it be a library book—or something left behind by the previous owners of the farmhouse?

In answering those questions, we need to remember one very important thing: We're not just seeing the book—we're seeing how the book looks to David. We're noticing what he notices, getting a sense of how it all makes him feel.

If you keep that in mind, you'll see that many of the words in the passage convey a sense of discomfort. The print is "smug," and the pages seem "like rectangles of dusty glass." From the start, before he reads a word of it, this book is vaguely upsetting to David. Its very appearance knocks him off balance.

Going further, I'd suggest that the description helps to convey David's feelings toward his parents—and, really, toward all adults. David doesn't like or trust adults, and he's not exactly eager to enter their world.

Look, for example, at the signature he finds in the front of the book. It's his mother's signature, you'll recall, and it's described as "upright," and "bold," and "careful"—a sharp contrast to the sloppy "backslant" he's used to seeing around the house.

These details give us the feeling that David is curious about his mother. What did she used to be like, and what happened to her? That's what he's asking here. How did this bold, confident young woman turn into my mom? How do I know that the same thing won't happen to me?

By now, I think, we can see why the book doesn't come from the library. But what if it had belonged to David's father? In that case, I suppose, you might be able to achieve much the same effect. But I think it works even better if it's the mother. The name in the book is her maiden name, after all—the name that she used before she had children, before she was married, maybe (who knows) before she'd even met David's father.

So even though we haven't gotten too far into "Pigeon Feathers," we've already learned something important: A good description not only helps to set the scene or create a vivid impression, it can also serve a larger purpose—helping us to understand how the world looks and feels to the characters. Remember, we don't just see the book, we see how it looks to David.

So what is in the book? What exactly does it say? It turns out this time you can judge a book by its cover. For this nasty, old book not only looks old and nasty—it also contains some very disturbing ideas.

You see, the book denies the divinity of Christ, describing Jesus as—and these words come straight from the story—"an obscure political agitator, a kind of hobo, in a minor colony of the Roman Empire."

 ©2009 The Teaching Company.

For David, this is simply inconceivable. Why would anyone ever say such a thing? How could anyone ever get away with it?

Before long, however, the book has gotten under David's skin. He can't stop thinking about it. What if it's true? What if Jesus was just "a kind of hobo"?

Interestingly, it's at this point that the story turns its attention from objects and things to people. It doesn't give us the full-on, head-to-toe description we might expect from Sir Walter Scott, but it does offer a good many striking details.

Let's go through them in order.

First, we see the waggling hands and wrinkled fingers of David's grandmother, who suffers from Parkinson's disease.

Then, we see the yellow skin of his father's eyelids.

Then, we see the grandmother again. This time it's not her hands, but her eyes—which seem to be "embedded in watery milk."

Then, it's back to the father: He "[does] not seem to have eyes at all," the narrator explains, "just jaundiced sockets of wrinkled skin."

These people are almost monstrous. They're more dead than alive. But as in the case of the book, we're not seeing them so much as we are seeing how they look to David.

By now it's clear that David is in crisis. Indeed, he's experiencing the sort of crisis we discussed in Lecture Four: the kind that happens when long-buried conflicts are forced to the surface.

You get the feeling, as you read the descriptions of David's family, that this isn't the first time he's noticed the waggling hands or the jaundiced eyelids. It may, however, be the first time he's really confronted the way he feels about those adult bodies.

All of this brings us to another very important point: You can't always deal with descriptions separately. Sometimes, you need to look for patterns or connections. If you do that here, you'll notice that the descriptions of the father and grandmother work to reinforce the earlier association of the ugly book (and its upsetting ideas) with the ugly, decaying adult world.

How does that work? Mostly, I think, through the subtle use of the color yellow: The father's eyelids are twice described as yellow and jaundiced, just like the edges of the pages of the book. That's pretty clever.

Taken together, all of these descriptions—the initial description of the book, and the later descriptions of the characters—raise another upsetting possibility: that the human body is nothing special; that it's really just another object, another thing. The bodies of David's relatives—his grandmother, his father—those bodies are clearly subject to disease and decay. They're already turning yellow, and they could easily start to smell—and eventually, they'll die. When they die, as David realizes in the very next scene, they'll be buried underground forever.

In that scene, David visits the outhouse, where he has a vision of death.

It's not a comforting vision, either. For David imagines that after death your body is thrown into a long hole. Once you're down there, your arms are pinned to your sides, and your face is covered with dirt.

"There you will be forever," he thinks, "blind and silent, and in time no one will remember you, and you will never be called."

So now we have a name for David's crisis: It's a spiritual crisis, a crisis of faith. He's afraid after reading this book and looking at his relatives that there's no such thing as heaven, no such thing as your immortal soul, no such thing as God.

How is his crisis resolved? Well, I won't tell you that. (I still feel bad about spoiling the end of that Chekhov story.) But I will tell you that the resolution is conveyed largely through detailed descriptions.

This time the descriptions focus on the bodies of animals—first, as a kind of prelude: There's a gorgeous description of the family dog, with an emphasis on how each hair is formed and colored.

Second—and this is the main event—there's a description of pigeon feathers. (You knew that had to come in there somewhere, right?)

Unlike the dog, these birds are dead. David has gone to clear them out of the barn with his shotgun. Still, the narrator is careful to say that their feathers "were more wonderful than the dog's hair."

Here's a bit of that description:

> He lost himself in the geometrical tides as the feathers now broadened and stiffened to make an edge for flight, now softened and constricted to cup warmth around the mute flesh. And across the surface of the infinitely adjusted yet somehow effortless mechanics of the feathers played idle designs of color, no two alike, designs executed, it seemed, in a controlled rapture, with a joy that hung level in the air above and behind him. Yet these birds bred in the millions and were exterminated as pests.

So is everything in the story described in such great detail? Interestingly, the answer is "No." For one very important thing is never described at all—that thing is David himself. We're told his age—over the course of the story, he turns 15—but that's it. We don't know if he's tall or short. We don't know what color his hair is or if he wears glasses.

In the end, then, David remains disembodied. In a very subtle way, he's exempted from the fate of those pigeons, the fate of his father and grandmother. Very interesting.

So, in addition to noticing what is described, you should also notice what isn't described. Whether a description is omitted on purpose or by accident, left out consciously or unconsciously, its absence can be very revealing.

Much of what we've learned from reading Updike will help us in dealing with our next author, Flannery O'Connor. Like Updike, O'Connor is a master of description. In her work, detailed description of people, places, and things—but most especially, people—is always an essential part of the drama.

For evidence in support of this claim, let's turn to a story called "Revelation." The initial setting for this story is the waiting room of a doctor's office. The waiting room is described in some detail, but as I've already suggested, most of our attention is focused on the people. Introduced first are the Turpins: Claud and his wife.

Mrs. Turpin is described first: She's "very large," and her "bright black eyes [take] in all the patients as she [sizes] up the seating situation."

Already we can sense that Mrs. Turpin will be a major character—and, indeed, we go on to see everyone and everything else in the waiting room through her "bright black eyes." She sees that there is only one vacant chair and—this is important—"a place on the sofa occupied by a blond child in a dirty blue romper who should have been told to move over and make room for the lady."

Got that? Not just a child, or even a blond child, but "a blond child in a dirty blue romper who"—and this is the kicker—"should have been told to move over and make room for the lady."

That's interesting. Where are those details coming from? Who says that the child was dirty and should have been told to make room for Mrs. Turpin? The author? The implied author? The third-person narrator? Of course not. The bit about moving over and making room for "the lady"—that comes from Mrs. Turpin herself. That's what she thinks, what she expects—she's the one who sees herself as a "lady." All of these details are conveyed to us through the skillful use of "free indirect discourse," the technique we examined back in Lecture Three.

As you'll recall, free indirect discourse allows a third-person narrator to move in and out of a character's mind without the use of cumbersome tags like "she thought" or "she said to herself." In this case, we're glad that O'Connor dispensed with those tags. If she had used them, she'd have slowed the flow of the paragraph and spoiled much of its humor.

So what general conclusions can we draw from O'Connor's initial descriptions? Like Updike, she seems to understand that it's better—more interesting—to show things from a particular point of view. So, as in Updike, we're not just seeing the waiting room and the dirty child—we are seeing how those things look to Mrs. Turpin.

Over the next six or seven pages, as the first part of the story unfolds, we're introduced to nine other characters—and each of them, like the dirty child, is seen and judged by Mrs. Turpin. In only one case— that of a "well-dressed, gray-haired lady"—is the judgment even remotely positive. Every other time, the description betrays Mrs. Turpin's feelings of social and moral superiority.

Here's exhibit A: "a fat girl of eighteen or nineteen, scowling into a … book." Her complexion is "blue with acne"; and Mrs. Turpin thinks "how pitiful it was to have a face like that at that age."

(Mrs. Turpin sees a bit of herself in this girl—both of them have problems with their weight—but she quickly takes comfort in the fact that she has always had "good skin.")

 ©2009 The Teaching Company.

Now for exhibit B: a "thin leathery old woman in a cotton print dress." Mrs. Turpin thinks she recognizes the origin of the dress, because she and her husband have—and let's make sure we get this exactly—"three sacks of chicken feed in their pump house that was in the same print."

(In addition to serving as another great example of free indirect discourse, the little grammatical slip at the end of that sentence helps in exploding Mrs. Turpin's social pretensions.)

Finally, exhibit C: "a lank-faced woman who was certainly the child's mother. … She had on a yellow sweat shirt and wine-colored [socks], both gritty looking," the narrator says, "and the rims of her lips were stained with snuff."

Mrs. Turpin freely labels this woman, and the older lady in the print dress, as "white-trashy." If you've ever lived in the South, you know what an insult that can be.

So, what can we take away from these examples? Quite a bit, really. For they show us that in some cases, descriptions don't simply add to the story—they tell the story. In a sense, they are the story.

Just look at the descriptions of these characters. Without all of those details—the cotton print dress, the snuff-stained lips, the skin blue with acne—the story would lose much of its vitality. More importantly, the characterization of Mrs. Turpin would lose much of its force.

It would be easy for the narrator to tell us that Mrs. Turpin is judgmental and self-righteous—but that wouldn't be nearly so much fun. No, it's more effective for the narrator to try and show us how often Mrs. Turpin rushes to judgment. We need to see this character in action. We need to see that, almost every time she sets eyes on a person, she looks for a reason to put them down.

O'Connor was never afraid to acknowledge that detailed descriptions, like the ones we've just seen, were vitally important to her work.

"The first and most obvious characteristic of fiction," she once said, "is that it deals with reality through what can be seen, heard, smelt, tasted, and touched."

With this statement, O'Connor admits that there are other ways of dealing with reality. The fiction writer's way, though, is through evocative descriptions: words and phrases that somehow engage or activate our senses.

Another one of her statements is worth considering here. For in this statement, O'Connor makes the sort of point we've been making throughout this lecture, insisting that the accumulation of detail is not an end in itself.

> [T]o say that fiction proceeds by the use of detail does not mean the simple, mechanical piling-up of detail [she says]. Detail has to be controlled by some overall purpose, and every detail has to be put to work for you. Art is selective. What is there is essential and creates movement.

These statements are wonderful—for they remind us that in a great story, details aren't simply "piled up." They're chosen or selected, carefully arranged and then put to work—all with a larger, controlling purpose in mind.

Fair enough. But what is the controlling purpose in this particular story? What is the point of the descriptions in "Revelation"? My sense is that O'Connor is using all of those details in a couple of ways. First, she wants us to see what Mrs. Turpin is like. Then—and this is a new point—she wants to trick us into behaving like Mrs. Turpin, trick us into being as dismissive and judgmental as this character can be. For only if O'Connor succeeds in playing that trick, only if she lures us into that trap, can she convince us that the story is something more than a comical look at a fat, foolish lady.

At first, this may not make much sense. In many ways, after all, we're not like Mrs. Turpin. We're intelligent, educated people, eager to master the art of reading, while she's the wife of a hog farmer. Her grammar is often atrocious—we've seen it for ourselves—and what's more, she reveals herself to be a racist and a snob. When you get right down to it, she's the trashy one—so how could anyone possibly think that she's at all like you and me?

Now do you see what I mean? We put her down, assume that she's beneath us—that's exactly what she does with almost every other person in the story. So, the story is not only about her—it's about us. If she's the target of O'Connor's satire—then so, my friends, are we.

Details and descriptions aid in the characterization of Mrs. Turpin. They also help to set a trap for us readers. For every time we read

 ©2009 The Teaching Company.

one of those descriptions, every time we condemn Mrs. Turpin for being judgmental, we run the risk of making the very same mistakes.

So what happens in the rest of the story? Once the cast has been assembled in that little waiting room, how does O'Connor set the plot in motion?

Well, if you must know, she has that fat girl—the one with the blue acne—attack Mrs. Turpin and call her a "wart hog from hell." That's right—a "wart hog from hell."

Has Mrs. Turpin done anything to provoke this assault? Yeah, sort of she has. She's been going on and on, making casually racist remarks and indicating her contempt for everyone else in the room. So although the attack is not justified, it is understandable.

Believe it or not, it makes a big impression on Mrs. Turpin—who, in many ways, takes it to heart. "I can't be a wart hog from hell," she says, "or can I?" This, then, is her spiritual crisis—her attempt to preserve a cherished self-image. She's always thought of herself as a kind, good, charitable Christian woman, and now she's forced to confront the possibility that she's actually ugly, and awful, and dirty.

She worries over this possibility for quite a while. The "wart hog" bit hits very close to home, since—as I mentioned earlier—her husband is a pig farmer. The story eventually makes its way to the pig pen, where Mrs. Turpin raises her voice in protest.

"Why me?" she asks. "How am I a hog? … Exactly how am I like them?"

She gets no answer—but she is granted a vision. It's the description of that final vision that concerns us now. The backdrop for the vision is beautiful, and so are the words used to describe it. "The sun is setting," the narrator says, "and there's a purple streak in the sky."

On this purple streak, Mrs. Turpin sees a "vast horde of souls … rumbling toward heaven."

As I read through the rest of the passage, please note the order of the procession. Mrs. Turpin has always assumed that she would go to heaven—and, moreover, that she would be near the front of the line. This time, however, things look different: "There were whole companies of white-trash, clean for the first time in their lives, and bands of black niggers in white robes, and battalions of freaks and lunatics shouting and clapping and leaping like frogs."

Obviously, a couple of things need to be said about this. The terms "white-trash" and "black niggers" come from Mrs. Turpin, not from the narrator or from O'Connor herself. They are offensive, and they're meant to be. But they are also the terms that Mrs. Turpin would use—indeed, she's used these words throughout the entire story—and we need to know that this is her vision.

Also worth considering is the term "freaks and lunatics." After the attack on Mrs. Turpin, the term "lunatic" is applied to that young woman with the acne—the young woman who jumps on Mrs. T. and calls her a "wart hog from hell." So, when we see that same word repeated in this passage, we're encouraged to think that the young woman may also have a place in the procession.

The passage goes on, and as it does, the description of the vision becomes even more powerful. For:

> bringing up the rear of the procession was a tribe of people whom she recognized at once as those who, like herself and Claud, had always had a little of everything and the God-given wit to use it right. She leaned forward to observe them closer. They were marching behind the others with great dignity, accountable as they had always been for good order and common sense and respectable behavior. They alone were on key. Yet she could see by their shocked and altered faces that even their virtues were being burned away.

This is the last image, the last bit of description, in O'Connor's last major story. It was published in 1964, the year of her death. As in the case of the Updike story, there's something that isn't described. This time, we don't hear what the people are wearing and don't really get a sense of what they look like.

That's because it no longer matters. It never has mattered—not to God, anyway. This is Mrs. Turpin's revelation, long promised and long delayed. Now she has a chance—and a choice. We don't know what she'll do. The ending is left open. But the more urgent question may be a question for us. What will we do? How will we receive this message?

©2009 The Teaching Company.

For both Updike and O'Connor, observation and description are not strictly literary matters—they have a spiritual dimension. Looking at things carefully, noticing all the details, can be a source of comfort—as it is for David in "Pigeon Feathers." Looking at things quickly, assuming that you already know what they mean—well, that can get you into trouble, as it does Mrs. Turpin in "Revelation."

To review, then: It's OK to skip descriptions when they seem formulaic or when they slow down the action, but skipping is not OK—or at least not advisable—in many other cases. In those cases, details are not merely presented—not merely piled up, as O'Connor explains.

They're presented from a particular point of view. They help us to see what the characters see—and invite us to rethink our own place in the story.

Are we like David? Are we so afraid of death that we see the human body as just another material object—another thing subject to change and decay? Or are we like Mrs. Turpin? Are we so convinced of our own moral virtue that we fall prey to smugness and sanctimony?

So, in conclusion: Sometimes the things that seem trivial, or cosmetic, or even ornamental—like passages of description—are directly connected to the largest, most urgent issues in fiction.

That seems like a good place for us to leave it. Thanks as always for joining us. We'll look forward to seeing you soon.

Lecture Six
Minimalists to Maximalists to Lyricists

Scope:

Style is often opposed to substance, as if stylishness were indistinguishable from superficiality. In this lecture, we will see what it really means to say that a writer is stylish. Our examples will come from the works of three influential American authors: Ernest Hemingway, William Faulkner, and F. Scott Fitzgerald. As we analyze the work of each author, we may also discover that their styles are more varied and flexible than we first thought; these styles make possible a wide range of meanings and effects.

Outline

I. What are the elements of style? Does style really make a difference? Which style is the best?

   A. We begin by noting a paradox: On one hand, stylish writers are thought to be gifted. On the other hand, great stylists are accused of working too hard.

   B. Our aim is to come up with better, more interesting ways of thinking about style.

   C. First we review the elements of style: diction and syntax. "Diction" means "word choice." "Syntax" means "word order."

   D. Though not everyone is stylish, everyone does have a style. No one style is better than the others.

   E. For some examples, we look at writers famous for their achievements as stylists: Ernest Hemingway, William Faulkner, and F. Scott Fitzgerald.

   F. As we look at each of those writers, we will ask if there is anything you can do with one style that you cannot do with the others.

II. We start with Hemingway. Our examples come from "Big Two-Hearted River."

   A. The main character is Nick Adams, who has come to northern Michigan to do some camping and fishing. He is trying to remain in control and focus on the here and now.

©2009 The Teaching Company.

B. For the task of following such a character and describing his situation, a minimalist style is a perfect choice.

C. Pay attention to the narrator's diction: The verbs are all one-syllable action verbs: slipped, lay, and looked.

D. As we look at Hemingway's style, we notice lots of other things: If he finds a good word, he is not afraid to repeat it. He also makes a point of using words that others might avoid.

III. If there are good reasons to be a minimalist, then why do all authors not use that style? This question takes us to Faulkner.

    A. His style is actually a natural outgrowth of his larger concerns, in particular his concern with history.

    B. Consider the case of Ike McCaslin in a short novel called *The Bear*. We look at a passage from the second paragraph of *The Bear*, in which Ike thinks back on past hunting trips.
        1. The first three sentences are short ones.
        2. The next sentence is a doozy, which reflects Ike thinking about the conversations that he heard or overheard on his earlier hunting trips.

    C. Did Faulkner have to write it up in this way?

    D. One final example from *The Bear* is from the very next sentence.
        1. This sentence begins like the last one.
        2. While we may have thought we had finished talking about the hunters' conversation, it turns out that topic is not yet exhausted.

    E. Despite the differences between Hemingway and Faulkner, there are at least two similarities.
        1. Both authors choose their styles deliberately.
        2. Both authors connect style and substance.

IV. Stylistic analysis can be both rewarding and fun.

    A. Find a writer whose style interests or intrigues you, and pick two or three pages at random and get started on a basic inventory.

    B. If you can get in the habit of asking questions about style, you will begin to appreciate the distinctive qualities of particular styles.

V. We take a quick look at F. Scott Fitzgerald, who works in a lyrical, or poetic, style.

    A. Fitzgerald uses many of the devices chiefly associated with the poetry of writers like Shakespeare and Keats.

    B. We can see a great example of Fitzgerald's poetic style as he introduces the title character at the very beginning of his novel *The Great Gatsby*.

Suggested Reading:

Mullan, *How Novels Work*, chap. 8.

Prose, *Reading like a Writer*, chaps. 1–3.

Questions to Consider:

1. What styles—besides the ones we have mentioned here—have you encountered in your recent reading? Which current writers seem to be working with the styles developed by Hemingway, Faulkner, and Fitzgerald?

2. Do you have your own style? If you looked back at all the things you have written in the last month—including interoffice memos and e-mails—would those writings have anything in common?

Lecture Six—Transcript
Minimalists to Maximalists to Lyricists

Hello, and welcome to Lecture Six in our course on the "art of reading."

This time, our topic is style. What are the elements of style? Does style really make a difference? Which style is the best? Those are the issues before us.

This should be a fun one, because it'll give us a chance to see how writers work—and play—with words. But I'm going to suggest that we begin by noting a paradox.

On one hand, stylish writers are thought to be gifted. They seem to have been blessed with an instinctive sense of how to put words together. They toss off beautiful expressions and memorable phrases almost effortlessly. They don't really need to think about it. To them, it just comes naturally.

On the other hand, great stylists are also accused of working too hard. They seem fussy. They sit and sit, constantly revising, worrying over little bits of language, when they should be getting on with more important tasks—like telling the story or developing the characters.

So if you're one of these stylish writers, you can't win for losing. Either you're a savant-like genius, endowed with almost freakish gifts—or you're an obsessive-compulsive, whose search for the perfect word or phrase makes no real difference in the end.

By now, it probably comes as no surprise to learn that neither of these stereotypes will work for us. For our aim is to come up with better, more interesting ways of thinking about style—and, as I mentioned earlier, to have fun doing it.

OK, then. Before doing anything else, let's run down the elements of style. That won't be terribly difficult because style really consists of only two things: diction and syntax.

Diction means "word choice." Does a writer prefer familiar, even common words—or does she like to go to her thesaurus every once in a while? Does she ever employ slang—or does she always remain somewhat formal? That's diction.

Syntax means "word order"—and, in this context, refers more generally to the arrangement or patterning of words. So, how long are most of your sentences? Do you stick with basic patterns—subject, verb, object—or do you like to mix things up every once in a while?

OK, then: diction and syntax—word choice and word order. Those are the elements of style. With that definition in place, we can lay out a few basic points.

Point number one: Though not everyone is stylish, everyone does have a style—a particular way of choosing and arranging words. It turns out, as a matter of fact, that even Morse Code operators have distinctive styles. Apparently if you're used to getting coded messages from two or three different people, and a new message comes in—you should be able to tell who sent it!

Point number two: Style is not the opposite of substance. Last time, we saw how description contributes to characterization. An apparently trivial or unnecessary feature of the work turned out to be crucially important.

It's the same way with style. For if a writer is any good at all, there's usually a close connection between style and substance. So, please don't fall into the trap of thinking that styles are chosen more or less at random. Style is not an add-on, like floor mats—it's standard equipment on this vehicle.

Point number three—and this is the last one: No style is better than the others. If you're skeptical about that, just ask yourself if a hammer is better than a monkey wrench. It all depends on what you're trying to accomplish, right? It's the same way with style. It all depends on your larger aims and purposes.

At this stage, we need some examples. I'm going to suggest that we look at writers famous for their achievements as stylists. I'm thinking here of Ernest Hemingway, William Faulkner, and F. Scott Fitzgerald—perhaps the greatest American novelists of the 20th century (the first half of it, anyway).

As many of you probably know, Hemingway is what we call a "minimalist." He prefers simple language and short sentences. Faulkner lies at the other end of the stylistic spectrum. I'd call him a "maximalist." He's famous for his complicated—some might say "convoluted"—sentences, which can go on for pages.

Fitzgerald? His style might be described as "poetic" or, more precisely, "lyrical." Though he's a fiction writer, he's obviously

©2009 The Teaching Company.

influenced by the great English poets—and he makes a point of employing the devices that they employed, paying close attention to sound effects and rhythmic patterns.

As we look at each of these writers, we'll try to figure out what their styles might be good for. In other words, we'll be asking if there's anything you can do with one style that you can't do—at least not as easily—with the others.

All right, then. Let's start with Hemingway. As we've noted, he's famous—perhaps notorious—for his use of short, simple sentences. Hemingway has been spoofed by everyone from E. B. White to Woody Allen. There's even a "Bad Hemingway Contest," which has been running for over 30 years now!

Nevertheless, there is no doubt that Hemingway's early stories are impressive achievements—and it's in these stories that he develops and refines his minimalist style.

Our examples will come from "Big Two-Hearted River," a two-part story published in the 1920s.

The main character—indeed, the only character—is Nick Adams. He's come to northern Michigan, all by himself, to do some camping and fishing.

Though the story doesn't say so directly, we sense that Nick is trying to get away from something. He almost seems to have been traumatized—and since the story was published in the '20s, it's easy to imagine that he's a veteran, back home from the war.

So in Nick Adams, Hemingway has a character who's trying—maybe struggling—to remain in control. He doesn't want to think or talk about the war. He needs to focus on the here and now.

For the task of following such a character and describing his situation, a minimalist style—focused on the here and now—is a perfect choice; for the minimalist style will suggest, in a way that other sorts of styles never could, the benefits of avoiding entanglement.

With all of that in mind, we're ready to look at a couple of examples from "Big Two-Hearted River."

Our first example comes from the first part of the story. Nick stops to rest—to take a little catnap—and the narrator describes his actions in the simplest way possible.

As I read this passage, pay attention to the narrator's diction. (That's word choice, right?) The verbs are all action verbs: "slipped," and "lay," and "looked." They're all one-syllable words, too.

With his choice of these words, the narrator suggests a desire to strip away abstractions, to shut down or shut off the mind and get back in touch with the body.

Interestingly, none of the verbs is modified. There are no adverbs here—it's "slipped," not "quickly slipped." Modifiers are unnecessary it seems, and maybe even wasteful.

OK, then. Here's the passage:

> Nick slipped off his pack and lay down in the shade. He lay on his back and looked up into the pine trees. His neck and back and the small of his back rested as he stretched. The earth felt good against his back. He looked up at the sky, through the branches, and then shut his eyes. He opened them and looked up again. There was a wind high up in the branches. He shut his eyes again and went to sleep.

Maybe it's just me—but that sounds nice. Nick is resting, stretching. Though he's connected to the earth, he's also looking up at the sky. He seems to be part of nature now. This is the feeling that he's been missing. This is why he's gone on this trip in the first place.

As we look at Hemingway's style, we might notice lots of other things: If he finds a good word, he's not afraid to repeat it. He doesn't go rushing after synonyms, mining the thesaurus for alternatives to his original choices.

He also makes a point of using words that others might avoid—the key example here being the word "good." For many writers, that word would be too common, too ordinary. Using it might even betray a lack of imagination. But Hemingway doesn't worry about any of that. He dares us to think of a better word than "good."

One more passage before we move on.

This is later on the same day, after Nick has set up camp.

As I read this one, note that the sentences are even shorter than before. There are 16 sentences in all here (I counted them myself), and none is more than 10 words long. Some are very short, indeed: 5 words, 6 words, even 3 words. (In case you're wondering, a scholar once determined that the average sentence in this story, "Big Two-Hearted River," is 12 words long.)

OK, so here goes:

> Nick was happy as he crawled inside the tent. He had not been unhappy all day. This was different though. Now things were done. There had been this to do. Now it was done. It had been a hard trip. He was very tired. That was done. He had made his camp. He was settled. Nothing could touch him. It was a good place to camp. He was there, in the good place. He was in his home where he had made it. Now he was hungry.

The first few sentences in this passage hint at Nick's experience of trauma. Why should a happy day be so unusual? Why is he used to feeling unhappy?

The last few sentences are interesting, too. Consider the patterning of these phrases: "a good place to camp"; "the good place"; and, finally, "home." As it goes along, things get simpler and simpler—more and more satisfying, too.

OK, then. If there are good reasons to be a minimalist, then why doesn't everyone use that style? Why doesn't everyone just write like Hemingway?

Those questions take us to Faulkner, the second of the writers on our list. He does appear to be Hemingway's polar opposite, and we might ask why he needs to go on, and on, and on—and on. Isn't his style a little self-indulgent?

Many critics have thought so. But if you look at Faulkner's writing closely, you'll see that his style—like Hemingway's—is not chosen at random. It's a natural outgrowth of his larger concerns, the most important of them being his concern with history.

Faulkner is a Southerner. He's from Mississippi. So he lives in a part of the country—a part of the world—where history is hardly ever forgotten. Many of his characters are descended from people who owned slaves or were slaves. Although the characters may try to shake off the burdens of the past, Faulkner doubts their ability to do so. As he once put it: "The past is never dead. It isn't even past."

For a better sense of what Faulkner is driving at, consider the case of Ike McCaslin, the central character in a short novel called *The Bear*. Ike is set to inherit the family estate, which he knows to have depended on slave labor. So what should he do with this knowledge? How can he live with it? What happens if he accepts the inheritance? Does that make him a party to the crimes of the slaveholders? What happens if he doesn't accept it? Does that mean that he's turning his back on his family?

It doesn't take long, then, for these things to get complicated—and it doesn't take long to see why minimalism just wouldn't work for Faulkner. He needs a style that allows him to explore the interpenetration of past and present, and that's exactly the sort of style that he uses in *The Bear*.

At this point, I'd like to take a look at a passage from the very beginning of *The Bear*.

This passage comes from the second paragraph, in which a 16-year-old Ike thinks back on the hunting trips he's been taking since the age of 10.

As I read, notice that the first three sentences are very short ones: 3 words, then 10, then 12. It almost sounds a bit like Hemingway: "He was 16. For six years now he had been a man's hunter. For six years now he had heard the best of all talking."

Before I go into the next sentence, which will be a doozy, let me offer one quick bit of advice. Remember that Ike is thinking about the conversations that he heard or overheard on his earlier hunting trips. The purpose of this next sentence, the long one, is to tell us what those old guys were talking about.

Are you ready? OK, here goes:

> It [that is, "the best of all talking"] was of the wilderness, the big woods, bigger and older than any recorded document— of white man fatuous enough to believe he had bought any fragment of it, of Indian ruthless enough to pretend that any fragment of it had been his to convey; bigger than Major de Spain and the scrap he pretended to, knowing better; older than old Thomas Sutpen of whom Major de Spain had had it and who knew better; older even than old Ikkemotubbe, the Chickasaw chief, of whom old Sutpen had had it and who knew better in his turn.

So these men, these hunters, not only talked about the woods and the wilderness, they made their hunting grounds seem bigger and older than any human being could ever be. This bit of wilderness is so big and so old that it mocks the people—like the "fatuous" white men or the "ruthless" Chickasaw Indians—who would presume to buy and sell it.

So far, so good. But did Faulkner really have to write it up in this way? Couldn't he have given us three or four shorter sentences instead?

Sure. But remember, Faulkner is obsessed with history. He thinks that it's always with us—that the past is never really past. So, he develops a style that makes our reading a little like wrestling with history. This style encourages us to notice patterns and make connections. More importantly, it asks us to look forwards and backwards at the very same time. For as we move into one of these long sentences, we have to keep looking back at the beginning of the sentence—and at earlier sentences, too. See how that works? It's very clever. As we move into the future, as we read through the sentence, we're not allowed to forget about the past.

I know that may seem rather abstract, so let me offer one final example from *The Bear*.

This example is the very next sentence, following directly after the ones we've just been discussing. Here's how it starts: "It was of the men."

Did you catch that? This sentence begins exactly like the last one, with the phrase "It was of." So while we may have thought we had finished talking about the hunters' conversation, it turns out that we were wrong. That topic is not yet exhausted. The past isn't even past.

OK, then. I'll start over, and this time I'll read the sentence all the way through to the end:

> It was of the men, not white nor black nor red but men, hunters, with the will and hardihood to endure and the humility and skill to survive, and the dogs and the bear and deer juxtaposed and reliefed against it, ordered and compelled by and within the wilderness in the ancient and unremitting contest according to the ancient and immitigable rules which voided all regrets and brooked no quarter;—the best game of all, the best of all breathing and forever the best of all listening, the voices quiet and weighty and deliberate

for retrospection and recollection and exactitude among the concrete trophies—the racked guns and the heads and skins—in the libraries of town houses or the offices of plantation houses or (and best of all) in the camps themselves where the intact and still-warm meat yet hung, the men who had slain it sitting before the burning logs on hearths when there were houses and hearths or about the smoky blazing of piled wood in front of stretched tarpaulins when there were not.

That's great stuff, and there is so much we could say about it. We could notice the way in which the shared experience of hunting erases racial difference. We could suggest that hunters are engaged in "ancient" rituals, and that talking about hunting is even better than actually hunting itself. We could suggest that Ike is being initiated into these rituals, taking his place in a community that stretches back to the beginning of human time.

We could do all of those things. What we really need to do now, though, is summarize. For despite the obvious differences between Hemingway and Faulkner, there are at least two important similarities.

First: Both authors choose their styles deliberately. None of this happens by accident.

Second: Both authors work hard to connect style and substance. In their work, when you get right down to it, style is substance.

By now, I hope you'll agree that stylistic analysis can be both rewarding and fun.

Try it for yourself, and you'll see what I mean. Find a writer whose style interests or intrigues you, and pick two or three pages at random—it'll probably work best if there isn't much dialogue—and get started on a basic inventory.

What kind of style are you dealing with? Is this writer a minimalist, a maximalist, or something else entirely? How many paragraphs do you see on each page? (You don't need an exact count, just a rough estimate.) How many sentences do you find in each paragraph? What about the sentences themselves? Do they tend to be long or short?

What about those elements of style: diction and syntax? What kinds of words are you hearing—are they long or short, familiar or esoteric—and how are those words arranged?

©2009 The Teaching Company.

If you can get in the habit of asking those questions—and, really, that's all we've been doing with Hemingway and Faulkner—you'll begin to appreciate the distinctive qualities of particular styles. You'll be reminded, yet again, of how much difference style can make.

OK, with the time we've got left, let's take a quick look at F. Scott Fitzgerald. He'll show us that minimalism and maximalism are not the only options—for as I noted when setting up this lecture, he works in a lyrical or poetic style.

What do I mean by that? Well, just that Fitzgerald uses many of the devices chiefly associated with the poetry of writers like Shakespeare and Keats. Such devices include rhythm and meter, as well as sound effects like alliteration and assonance.

Before moving on, I should explain that "alliteration" is the term we use to describe the repetition of initial consonant sounds—as in the old tongue twister: "Peter Piper picked a peck of pickled peppers." "Assonance" is a less familiar term. We use it to talk about the repetition of vowel sounds. A few quick examples of assonance might be "nice tie," or "good book," or "please leave."

We can see a great example of Fitzgerald's poetic style at the very beginning of his most famous novel, *The Great Gatsby*.

In this passage, the narrator, a young man named Nick Carroway, is describing the title character for the first time.

> If personality is an unbroken series of successful gestures, then there was something gorgeous about him, some heightened sensitivity to the promises of life, as if he were related to one of those intricate machines that register earthquakes ten thousand miles away. This responsiveness had nothing to do with that flabby impressionability which is dignified under the name of the "creative temperament"—it was an extraordinary gift for hope, a romantic readiness such as I have never found in any other person and which it is not likely I shall ever find again.

That is gorgeous, isn't it? This is the sort of thing that makes people fall in love with Fitzgerald. For richness of language, sheer sensual pleasure, he's unsurpassed.

I'm going to read this paragraph again in a minute, and as I do, please listen for the use of sound effects. At the beginning, you'll hear lots of "s" sounds and some "g" sounds, too. There aren't many "p" sounds here, but when they appear, they make a big impression (just listen for "personality" and "promises").

As the paragraph unfolds, new sounds are carefully introduced. Consider, for example, a phrase like "flabby impressionability"—or, in a different key, "romantic readiness." This really is a bit like a musical texture, working through repetition and variation. See if you can hear what I mean as I read the passage again:

> If personality is an unbroken series of successful gestures, then there was something gorgeous about him, some heightened sensitivity to the promises of life, as if he were related to one of those intricate machines that register earthquakes ten thousand miles away. This responsiveness had nothing to do with that flabby impressionability which is dignified under the name of the "creative temperament"—it was an extraordinary gift for hope, a romantic readiness such as I have never found in any other person and which it is not likely I shall ever find again.

In some of my earlier remarks on Fitzgerald, I said that in addition to working with sound effects, he pays close attention to rhythm and meter. If you're having trouble with that point, try a phrase like this one: "an unbroken series of successful gestures"—or: "one of those intricate machines." Can you hear it now?

I'm not asking you to work through the meter exactly. I just want you to look for some sort of fairly regular pulse.

Let's try it again. This time, we'll work with another phrase: "some heightened sensitivity to the promises of life." That's "some heightened sensitivity to the promises of life."

Here, the rhythm is almost perfectly iambic, especially if you run "to" and "the" together a little bit—and that sort of thing is not against the rules, by the way. Shakespeare and Keats, they do it all the time. Do you know what I mean by "iambic"? I should probably explain that, too. That's when syllables are alternated in this way: unstressed, stressed, unstressed, stressed, and so on.

Now can you hear that sort of rhythm in "some heightened sensitivity to the promises of life"? It's pretty obvious, I think, when

 ©2009 The Teaching Company.

he gets to "the *prom*is*es* of *life*." But it's also there at the beginning, when he's taking you through "some *height*ened *sen*si*tivity*."

Why is that worth noting? To me, it's like finding a little bit of Mozart or Chopin in the middle of a Barry Manilow tune. Here, as Fitzgerald is introducing the title character in a popular novel, something that we might tend to look on rather skeptically, he gives us a quick hit of Shakespeare and Keats. He lets us know that he's an ambitious writer. In so doing, he owns up to his own largest aspirations. From this point on it's clear: He's not just telling a story—he wants this book to be a thing of beauty. I'm not sure if Barry Manilow ever reached that high.

One last passage from Fitzgerald, mostly because I can't resist. Here, Nick imagines a crucial moment from Gatsby's past: his first kiss with Daisy Fay, Nick's second cousin, later the wife of a man named Tom Buchanan:

> His heart beat faster and faster as Daisy's white face came up to his own. He knew that when he kissed this girl, and forever wed his unutterable visions to her perishable breath, his mind would never again romp like the mind of God. So he waited, listening for a moment longer to the tuning-fork that had been struck upon a star. Then he kissed her. At his lips' touch she blossomed for him like a flower and the incarnation was complete.

So Gatsby can have this first kiss with Daisy, or he can look forward to the kiss—but he can't do both. Put another way, he's caught between the body (think here of "incarnation") and the mind or the spirit (romping "like the mind of God"). This sort of experience, we feel, can only be conveyed through poetry—and so once again, Fitzgerald offers gorgeous sound effects and irresistible rhythms.

In closing this lecture, we might return to one of the points raised at the beginning. No one style is better than the others. Like the hammer or the monkey wrench, the different styles of our three writers are designed for different uses, different purposes. Just as you wouldn't use a hammer to tighten a bolt, you probably wouldn't use Hemingway's style to describe Gatsby's first kiss with Daisy—or, for that matter, Ike McCaslin's memories of those childhood hunting trips.

One last bit of fun before we wrap this one up completely, because I think this little exercise will help you to see what it's actually like to experiment with different styles. So, please imagine what would happen if Hemingway, Faulkner, and Fitzgerald tried to describe the same basic act: Let's say that it's feeding the dog.

How would Hemingway describe the act of feeding the dog? What about Faulkner or Fitzgerald? What kind of language would they use? What kind of groove would they eventually get into? Here are my guesses.

Hemingway: "The bowl felt cold. It was heavy against his hand."

Faulkner:

> This was the feeding of Penny, the little Wheaton Terrier with the twinkle in her deep brown eyes, hungrier and fussier than any dog he had ever raised—hungrier than the too-tall schnauzer, Poppy, bred by his mother's uncle and shipped up to their family from St. Louis.

Finally, Fitzgerald: "If feeding a dog is a daily ritual, it is one possessed of an undeniable sense of communion—a communion between species, between people eager for love and companionship and eager, ardent little beasts, invariably desperate for dinner."

I'll stop there. But I hope that you'll try this game for yourself some time—and when you do, pick something equally mundane: Washing dishes would be another good choice. You'll have a good time with it—I promise—and you'll come away with an even better sense of what a big difference style can make.

Thanks as always for joining us. We'll look forward to seeing you soon.

 ©2009 The Teaching Company.

Lecture Seven
Explosive Devices—Irony and Ambiguity

Scope:

Irony is one of the most important terms in the entire literary lexicon—and also, as it happens, one of the most elusive. We start this lecture with a simple, straightforward definition of irony: If there is a discrepancy between what you say and what you mean, you are probably being ironic. The most common form of irony is sarcasm ("nice tie"), but it is the subtler, more complex forms that will concern us here. Exploring the effects of irony reveals the powerful and enduring connection between irony and ambiguity: As we will see in our readings of Mansfield stories like "Bliss," ambiguity is the end result—and indeed, the desired result—of an ironic approach to storytelling.

Outline

I.   Our subjects for this lecture are irony and ambiguity. I am labeling irony and ambiguity as "explosive" because they explode all kinds of things, including vanity, pretension, and self-righteousness.

II. We begin with "Bliss," the title story in Katherine Mansfield's second collection.

    A. Let me start with Mansfield's title. What should we expect from a story called "Bliss"?

    B. The possibility of irony is reinforced by the name of the central character: Bertha Young (who is 30 years old).

    C. With this in mind, we look at the opening paragraph. There seems to be an ironic discrepancy between the title and the rest of the story.

    D. "Bliss" is an interesting and tricky case. One complicating factor is the narrator's heavy use of free indirect discourse, which makes it harder for us to tell what the narrator thinks.

    E. The title, the name of the central character, and the opening paragraphs—with their heavy use of free indirect discourse—all point in the direction of irony.

III. I hope you have noticed my heavy use of the word "discrepancy."

IV. It is time for us to move on to the new terminology.

    A. Verbal irony is what you get when words do not quite match their uses. Dramatic irony is a discrepancy between the characters and the reader or the audience.

    B. We deal with different kinds of irony in very different ways. Stable irony is usually a matter of simple reversal, where there is no doubt about the meaning or intention. In cases of unstable irony, we never reach a final conclusion, though we detect the presence of irony.

V. We shrink the term "irony" back down again and start to look for possible connections to ambiguity.

    A. The best way to shrink irony back down is by applying some of our new terminology to "Bliss."

    B. Bertha's last line is completely open ended, and that is where our second device, ambiguity, really comes into play.

VI. What else have we learned from the story—and from the lecture as a whole?

    A. There is more than one kind of irony, and several different kinds may be present in the same story.

    B. Some ironies may be obvious at first, and others may not emerge until a second or third reading.

    C. Some ironies are relatively easy to deal with, while others may never be resolved completely.

    D. In the case of the most unstable ironies, the end result may be a larger sense of ambiguity or open-endedness.

    E. I might note one further irony: Bertha's final question is the same question that we ask whenever we pick up a book or a story.

Suggested Reading:

Booth, *A Rhetoric of Irony*.

Muecke, *Irony*.

Questions to Consider:

1. It is often said that we are living in an age of irony: No one takes anything seriously; everyone adopts an attitude of detachment or disengagement; and so on. Do you think that is true? And if so, why do you suppose that would be?

2. Is it possible for a story to be too ambiguous? Do you find yourself getting impatient with authors like Mansfield, or do you admire their refusal to settle for easy answers?

Lecture Seven—Transcript
Explosive Devices—Irony and Ambiguity

Hello, and welcome to Lecture Seven in our course on the "art of reading."

This time our subject is irony—and the closely related phenomenon of ambiguity. Of all the subjects we've covered so far, these may be the trickiest.

Why? Well, for one thing, authors seldom announce their intention to be ironic or ambiguous. They're just not inclined to issue an "irony alert" or an "ambiguity warning." So, there will be times when even the most experienced reader will feel somewhat unsure of herself.

At these times, the reader will sense that the author is hinting at something—but not really stating it directly. So, the reader will wonder if she's right to pick up on those hints. Am I on to something here? Or am I just confused?

We've all been there. We've all found ourselves in the middle of a paragraph—or maybe even a sentence—that seems just a little slippery. That's why we need some help in learning how to detect the presence of irony and ambiguity.

Unfortunately, there is no foolproof test. But with just a little bit of practice, you can begin to heighten your sensitivity to the presence of irony and ambiguity. When you develop some confidence in your ability to recognize these devices, you should be able to see why I'm labeling them as "explosive."

They explode all kinds of things, in my opinion—including vanity, pretension, and self-righteousness. Once the dust from the explosion settles, our illusions have been cleared away—and we've been put back in touch with reality.

I think that's enough to get us started. Looking ahead to the rest of the lecture, I can tell you that this one will have three parts.

In Part 1, we'll begin to get some practice in the detection of irony. Here, we'll be looking at the opening of a classic short story by Katherine Mansfield. (The title of the story, by the way, is "Bliss.")

Later, in Part 2, we'll learn some new vocabulary—and begin to explore the relationship between irony and ambiguity.

©2009 The Teaching Company.

Finally, in Part 3, we'll try to bring it all together. Our main aim here will be to see what our new terms and concepts might add to our reading of "Bliss."

Let's begin, then, with Katherine Mansfield. If she's not familiar to you, that's OK—because she doesn't always get the attention she deserves. She died young, and her output was relatively slim: just three collections of short stories.

But let me assure you that Mansfield's achievements in the form of the short story are thoroughly impressive. She was a contemporary of early 20th-century writers like D. H. Lawrence and Virginia Woolf, and they thought very highly of her. As a matter of fact, Woolf once identified Mansfield as the only writer she was ever jealous of.

As we move through the rest of the lecture, we'll see why Woolf had good reason to be jealous of Katherine Mansfield. More importantly, we'll gain some experience in the detection of irony.

Let's start at the very beginning—with Mansfield's title. We haven't talked about titles yet, and this will be a great opportunity to do so.

In many cases, a story or novel is named after one of the characters—"Young Goodman Brown"; "The Lady with the Dog"; *The Great Gatsby*. In other cases, the title points us toward a crucial image—"Pigeon Feathers" or *The Bear*.

In this case, the story takes its name from a feeling—and not just any feeling, but bliss: an especially intense feeling; a feeling of complete joy and perfect happiness; a feeling unalloyed by fear, anxiety, or regret.

So what should we expect from a story called "Bliss"? At this point, we don't quite know. Several possibilities do seem to be in play, however.

It's possible that the story will center on some wonderful, blissful event. Maybe this will be the story of a wedding or the birth of a child. That would be nice—a little boring, I suppose, but nice.

That's not the only possibility, however. Bliss is, after all, an unusual feeling. Indeed, we might wonder if bliss can ever be experienced on earth, ever be experienced in this life. We're all familiar with the term "heavenly bliss," right? That term certainly does suggest that bliss is only available to us in the afterlife.

If that's true, then perhaps there will turn out to be some discrepancy between the title and the rest of the story. Perhaps this will actually turn out to be a story of failure and disappointment. Perhaps the characters will reach for sheer joy—for perfect happiness, for bliss—and somehow fall short.

Notice what we're doing here. We're looking for irony, but we're not applying a litmus test. We're not running down a checklist. We're just playing with words, asking questions about them: So what do I make of this word "bliss"? Where have I seen the word before? What does the word usually mean? Is there a chance that it's supposed to have some other sort of meaning in this situation?

When you ask those questions, you're activating your own built-in irony detector. Right now, that thing should be flashing—maybe not red, but yellow, for there's a fairly good chance that the title and the story will not fit together in the end.

The possibility of irony is also reinforced by the name of the central character: Bertha Young. (Now that I think of it, we haven't said anything about names, either—so this is another great opportunity for us.)

Bertha's name is given in the very first sentence—and so, for that matter, is her age, which is 30. So, although her name is "Young," Bertha is past the first blush of youth. She's not old—by a long shot—but she's not a kid, either.

When you think about it, 30 may be the perfect age for Bertha. If she were 20 or 25, her name would actually be quite appropriate. If she were 40 or 50, the discrepancy between her name and her age would be too obvious, too unsubtle. No, 30 is exactly the right choice.

To sum up, then: Both the title and the name point in the direction of irony. In both cases, we're dealing with some kind of discrepancy: a possible discrepancy between the title and the rest of the story; a more obvious discrepancy between Bertha's name and her actual situation.

With all of that in mind, we're ready to look at the opening paragraph. As I read through it, be on the lookout for other possible signs of irony. Here goes:

> Although Bertha Young was thirty she still had moments like this when she wanted to run instead of walk, to take

©2009 The Teaching Company.

dancing steps on and off the pavement, to bowl a hoop, to throw something up in the air and catch it again, or to stand still and laugh at—nothing—at nothing, simply.

Well, what do you think? Is Bertha's life a blissful one? Maybe. She does experience moments of intense pleasure and great satisfaction—and yet, at the same time, maybe not.

For one thing, she seems to be trying a bit too hard. She's willing her happiness into being, instead of letting it emerge more naturally.

In addition, she may be doing some of this for show. Does she want others to see and admire her youthful exuberance—to notice how different she is from other women her age? It's hard not to get that feeling.

So, in this first paragraph, we begin to detect yet another discrepancy: a discrepancy between Bertha's vision of herself and our view of her. Where she sees herself as a free spirit, we're inclined to see her as needy and anxious.

By now, it should be clear that "Bliss" will be an interesting and tricky case. One complicating factor is the narrator's heavy use of "free indirect discourse." That's the device we've seen a couple of times before—the one we've linked to writers like Gustave Flaubert and Flannery O'Connor.

In a passage of free indirect discourse—or, as we say in the trade, "f.i.d."—a third-person narrator seems to take or borrow her language from one of the characters. We saw that happen with Madame Bovary, and now we're seeing it again with Bertha.

Where exactly do we see it?

In phrases like "stand still and laugh at—nothing—at nothing, simply." Those phrases have the texture, the feel, of actual speech. They sound like the kinds of phrases we'd hear from Bertha if we were talking with her over lunch.

How are things complicated by the use of f.i.d.? Well, for one thing, f.i.d. makes it harder for us to tell what the narrator thinks. To get at the narrator—not to mention the implied author—we have to get through Bertha. That's just not easy to do.

To see what I mean, just ask yourself a few simple questions: Does the narrator want us to admire Bertha's youthful exuberance? Or is she inviting us to think of Bertha as needy and anxious? What is the narrator's "take" on the story's main character?

At this point, there's only one way to find out—and that, of course, is to read further. So, here's the second paragraph.

As I read this one, listen for the narrator's continued use of free indirect discourse. It will be even more obvious here. Think about the gap between our view of Bertha and Bertha's vision of herself. Is the gap beginning to narrow—or is it getting wider?

Ready? OK, then. Here we go:

> What can you do if you are thirty and, turning the corner of your own street, you are overcome, suddenly, by a feeling of bliss—absolute bliss!—as though you'd suddenly swallowed a bright piece of that late afternoon sun and it burned in your bosom, sending out a little shower of sparks into every particle, into every finger and toe?

You probably noticed that this paragraph takes us straight back to the title. Indeed, the paragraph employs the word "bliss" not just once, but twice.

You've probably also concluded that the paragraph widens the gap between us and Bertha. This time, the language is not merely forced or strained—but way over the top. This time, it's clear that Bertha is trying way too hard to appear sensitive or poetic. Just look at phrases like "suddenly swallowed" or "burned in your bosom." Something there is not quite right. Something there is not exactly blissful.

So by now, your irony detector should be flashing red. The title, the name, the use of f.i.d. in the first two paragraphs, the overblown language in those paragraphs—just about every element of the story is pointing you in the direction of irony.

I hope that this first part of the lecture has given you a better sense of how to detect the presence of irony. As we've seen, the detection of irony often proceeds slowly. There may not be a single, dramatic "aha moment"—a point where everything suddenly snaps into place. It's more likely that your perception of irony will develop gradually—that you will need to test and revise your assumptions as you move along.

I hope you've also noticed a few other things—including my repeated use of the word "discrepancy." I've been making a big deal

©2009 The Teaching Company.

of that word, and that's because it often figures into discussions or definitions of irony.

When defining irony, most scholars point to discrepancies like the ones we've begun to notice in "Bliss": The title doesn't fit with the rest of the story, or the characters' views are not quite in line with our own.

Scholars of irony also point to what we might call "the mother of all discrepancies"—the big one, "the burninator"—and that is the familiar Platonic distinction between appearance and reality.

In my opinion, that only makes sense. As we catch on to the presence of irony, we begin to feel that we're discovering the truth—getting in touch with reality. This, it seems to me, is exactly what Plato wants for his students and his readers. He wants us to look beyond conventional wisdom—to think for ourselves, to see how things really are.

We're into the second part of the lecture now, and it's time for us to deepen and sharpen our vision of irony. I promised that this part would include some new terminology, so let me start with two key concepts: "verbal irony" and "dramatic irony."

As you might expect, verbal irony has something to do with words. In fact, verbal irony is what you get when your words don't quite match their uses. The most familiar kind of verbal irony is sarcasm.

If, after we're done taping, the cameraman comes up to me and says: "Nice tie," there's a pretty good chance he means just the opposite. If so, then he's engaging in verbal irony.

Obviously, there are other forms of verbal irony. Take another look at Mansfield's language or her title, and you'll see what I mean. The title is ironic—it doesn't quite mean what it says, but we wouldn't say that it's also sarcastic. For one thing, it's just a lot more complicated, a lot more difficult to figure out, than something like "Nice tie."

So that, in a nutshell, is verbal irony. What about dramatic irony? That's the sort of thing you might see not only in a book, but also in a play or a movie. We're dealing with another discrepancy here—but this time it's a discrepancy between the characters and the reader or the audience. Simply put, the characters assume that the situation is one way, and we know that they're dead wrong.

The standard examples of dramatic irony come from Greek tragedy—and more specifically, from *Oedipus the King*: Oedipus vows to find out who killed the previous king; the audience, already familiar with the story, knows that he is the killer—and that the previous king also happened to be his father.

So, we've got verbal irony and dramatic irony: ironic language and ironic action. But that doesn't exhaust the subject, for there are at least two other terms for us to consider: "stable irony" and "unstable irony."

These terms were coined by Wayne C. Booth. His name should sound familiar, since he's the man who brought you the "implied author" back in Lecture Two. With stable and unstable irony, Booth gives us a way to distinguish among different sorts of verbal irony. What's more, he calls attention to the reading process, noting that we deal with different kinds of irony in very different ways.

Stable irony is relatively easy for us to deal with. In a case of stable irony, it's usually a matter of simple reversal: He says my tie is "nice," and I realize he means just the opposite. Once I come to that realization, my work as a reader or interpreter is done. I may not like the end result—I don't see what's wrong with this tie—but I have no doubt that I've captured his meaning or understood his intention.

You can probably see where this is going. In cases of unstable irony, we never reach a final conclusion. Oh, we detect the presence of irony, and we may be able to identify a range of possible meanings. But, try as we might, we just can't decide which of those meanings is the right one. So, the situation is not only unstable—but also likely to remain that way.

In describing such situations, Booth speaks of "a possibly infinite series of further confusions." As you can tell, he doesn't much like that kind of thing—and it's important for us to see that he doesn't blame the reader for any of it. It's not that we need to work harder or think more clearly. It's the author who's at fault—according to Booth, I mean—the author who refuses to take or even imply a final position on the issues raised by the story. That's where Booth takes this argument.

I think he's got a point there. Certainly, I can think of authors who seem to abdicate their responsibilities. I can also think of a few who enjoy jerking their readers around. But I sometimes get the sense that Booth wants to reserve the designation "unstable irony" for the really extreme cases—and I don't always feel like following him there.

 ©2009 The Teaching Company.

Whether I'm right about that or not, I do feel sure that our vocabularies could be expanded even further. We could, for example, talk about "romantic irony." This term may seem to describe the experience of falling in love—but, in fact, it has nothing to do with that sort of thing. It refers instead to a set of ideas first advanced in Germany at the beginning of the 19th century—the Romantic Period—and it gets at the conflicted feelings that artists may have toward their own work.

We could also discuss the idea of "cosmic irony." This one has to do with our place in the universe. Why did God make us this way? Why have our noble spirits been cooped up in these mortal bodies? Are we put here just to suffer and die? If these questions have some resonance for you, then you may want to find out more about cosmic irony.

Finally, we could look at the sort of irony described by the late Richard Rorty, perhaps the most important American philosopher of the last 40 years. For Rorty, an "ironist" is the sort of person who, though committed to a particular worldview, is also impressed by other views and inclined to think that conflicts among such views can never be completely resolved. He felt that the world could use more ironists, and in his later books he tried to explain why. If you're interested in that project, you might start with a book called *Contingency, Irony, and Solidarity*, which Rorty published in 1989.

So, in this part of my lecture—the second part—we've learned some new vocabulary. We should also have gotten the idea that irony is a very elastic term, one that stretches far enough to cover issues of aesthetics (romantic irony), religion (cosmic irony), and epistemology (that's Rorty's kind of irony).

As we move into the third and final part of the lecture, let's try to shrink the term "irony" back down to size again. Let's start to look for possible connections to another important term—namely, "ambiguity."

The best way to shrink irony back down to size, in my opinion, is by applying some of our new terminology to "Bliss," the short story we were discussing at the beginning of the lecture. We've already noticed the presence of verbal irony in that story—but what about dramatic irony? That's the sort of thing you get in *Oedipus*, where the audience knows something that the characters don't.

I think that dramatic irony is present in "Bliss." From the very start, we sense that Bertha Young is heading for trouble. She wants a blissful life, a taste of heaven on earth, and we have a sinking feeling that she's not going to get it. Eventually, we suspect, things will come crashing down on her. It's inevitable—only a matter of time.

Interestingly, we get an even stronger sense of dramatic irony on a second reading. To explain how that works, I'll need to tell you the end of the story. I'm sorry about that—but remember, it's for a good cause.

OK. At the very end of the story—and I mean in the last two pages—Bertha discovers that her husband is having an affair with one of her friends. This discovery comes as a complete surprise to her—and it surprises us, too.

It happens at the end of a party hosted by Bertha and her husband. The party is breaking up, and Bertha's friend (Miss Fulton) moves toward the door. Bertha gets up to see her out—only to find her husband rushing past her.

She thinks nothing of it and returns to a conversation with another one of their guests. When she looks up, she sees her husband helping Miss Fulton with her coat. Suddenly, he tosses off the coat, turns Miss Fulton around, and looks at her with "a hideous grin." (That comes straight from the story, by the way.)

He whispers: "Tomorrow," and Miss Fulton seems to say: "Yes."

What a blow—and what a complete reversal. Just a few hours earlier, while Bertha was getting ready for the party, she had enjoyed a feeling of bliss. She'd been feeling proud of herself, perfectly content with her life—and now …

There's a further irony here: For as the party was just beginning to wind down—just before Miss Fulton got up to leave—Bertha had experienced a sudden rush of sexual desire for her husband.

They've been married a long time, and they've had a child together. She's always felt a great deal of affection for him, maybe even love for him.

But she's never before felt anything like this. She's never before wanted him so "ardently." She wonders if her new sexual passion isn't "what that feeling of bliss had been leading to." (That's from the story as well.)

On a first reading, Bertha's desire for her husband may seem like yet another example of her foolishness. But on a second reading, with the foreknowledge of his adultery, it looks very different. Now, it's horribly sad—maybe even heartbreaking.

So, near the end, this story presents us with a textbook example of dramatic irony. Bertha doesn't see what's coming, but we do. It's just like Oedipus vowing to find out who killed the king.

What we see here, I think, is both interesting and instructive—for this example shows that not all ironies come into focus at the same time. Sometimes it takes a second reading—and if it does, that's OK.

It may be that the story is actually designed for multiple readings: You see it one way the first time through, and then—on later readings—you see it differently. I suspect that's what Mansfield was going for in "Bliss."

So, we've made some headway with verbal and dramatic irony. Now what about stable and unstable irony? How do those terms apply to this story?

In pursuing that question, we'll need to make a choice. We'll need to decide if the central irony in the story—that is, the ironic presentation of Bertha—is stable or unstable? It will have to be one or the other. This time, we can't have it both ways.

If it were up to me, I'd go with unstable—though for reasons I've already noted, I'm not sure that Wayne Booth would agree. I do not see a "possibly infinite series of confusions" here—don't get me wrong—but I do see a lot of possible confusions, and I'm not sure I know how I'm supposed to resolve them.

Let me put it this way: Mansfield's portrayal of Bertha is—ready for this?—ambiguous. Even if you know the ending, and even if you've read the story multiple times, it remains very difficult—maybe even impossible—to reach a final, conclusive judgment about Bertha.

She is foolish, anxious, and self-deluded. It's hard not to laugh at her at times, but it's also hard not to feel sorry for her, too. She's a victim of her husband's treachery—and a victim of her friend's disloyalty as well.

What's more, her last line—which is practically the last line in the entire story—is completely open-ended. That's where our second device, ambiguity, really comes into play.

According to my dictionary, an ambiguous word or statement is one that can be interpreted in at least two ways. In thinking about Bertha's last line, I'd go even further, arguing that it invites—and may, indeed, require—multiple interpretations.

So what exactly does Bertha say? "Oh, what is going to happen now?" That's it. "Oh, what is going to happen now?"

At this point, the narrator doesn't tell us anything else. There's no free indirect discourse. It's just this line of dialogue. That line can be interpreted in so many ways—it's deeply, deeply ambiguous—and there's no way to determine which of those interpretations is the right one. Does Bertha feel like a fool? If so, you couldn't blame her—and yet, how could she have seen what her husband was up to? He covered his tracks pretty well.

Has Bertha given up on the idea of bliss? If so, how are we supposed to feel about her decision? Are we glad that she's finally facing reality, finally acting her age? Or are we saddened by the thought that she's been broken by this experience? Wouldn't we feel better if she could retain some small measure of hope?

All of those questions are left hanging at the end—every single one of them. So, in addition to providing some great examples of irony, this story offers a terrific example of ambiguity.

What else have we learned from the story—and indeed, from the lecture as a whole? Well, for starters, that there's more than one kind of irony—and that several different kinds may be present in the very same story. Some may be obvious at first. Others may not emerge until a second or a third reading.

We've also learned that some ironies are relatively easy to deal with, while others may never be resolved completely. In the case of the most-unstable ironies, the end result may be a larger sense of ambiguity or open-endedness. As Bertha herself might put it: "Oh, what is going to happen now?"

Before signing off, I might note one final irony: Bertha's last question—it's the same question that we ask whenever we pick up a book or a story to read. So, in a very subtle way, although the ending may appear to place us outside the situation—by refusing us access to Bertha's inner life (remember, there's no free indirect discourse there), it actually puts us down in the middle of it.

 ©2009 The Teaching Company.

At its best, that's how irony works. It explodes our own sense of superiority to the characters and reminds us of how difficult it can be to make sense of the world—to deal with that age-old discrepancy between appearance and reality. If someone were looking down on us and telling the story of our lives, there's a good chance that it would be ironic, too.

Thanks as always for joining us. We'll look forward to seeing you soon.

Lecture Eight
Reading for the Plot—Five Simple Words

Scope:

In the next two lectures, we will turn our attention to the crucial issue of narrative structure. As we grapple with this issue, we will need to consider some very tricky questions. What tends to happen at the beginning of a story? What has to happen before a story can end? And what holds a story together, giving it a larger sense of coherence and direction? Our pursuit of these questions will take us in two very different directions.

Outline

I. We are now ready to deal with plot in some detail.

    A. Plot is the story: the arc, shape, or structure of the piece.

    B. This is an enormous subject, but for now, we focus our attention on the essentials.

    C. We need to remember five words: "beginning," "middle," "end," "plot," and "story."

    D. By the end of this lecture, we will see what the words mean, find out where they come from, and gain a better sense of what they can do for you.

II. I want you to look for larger patterns, to notice underlying shapes and overarching structures.

    A. Our example will be "A Temporary Matter," the first story in Jhumpa Lahiri's *The Interpreter of Maladies*.

    B. We begin with "beginning," "middle," and "end."

        1. Those words come to us from Aristotle's *Poetics*.

        2. Much of the *Poetics* is devoted to the subject of plot.

    C. Aristotle makes some very interesting points.

        1. A plot is not unified simply because it relates the experiences of a single person.

        2. In a well-made plot, nothing can be eliminated, transposed, or rearranged.

        3. Each new event should happen because of—not just after—the earlier events.

4. Behind all of Aristotle's points, we can discover a disdain for episodic plots.

D. In moving from Aristotle's general rules to our particular example, we see that Lahiri's plot is by no means episodic.

    1. There are six sections in the story, and if you eliminated any one of them, the entire structure would collapse.

    2. If you rearranged the sections, it would change the entire mood and feeling of the story. Instead of "What is wrong?" the story makes us ask "What is next?"

III. What does Aristotle have to say about "beginning," "middle," and "end"?

A. Beginnings: What are they, and how do they work?

    1. At the beginning, we are introduced to the characters and their situation—which, at this point, is relatively stable.

    2. But before long, a destabilizing event occurs, and it knocks the characters off balance, preventing them from going on with life as usual.

    3. Lahiri's beginning features two destabilizing events, pulling in opposite directions: separation and renewed connection. There is the death of the baby and the arrival of a notice from the power company that forces the couple out of their regular routine.

B. The middle is where complications arise, and we get a better sense of what the characters are up against.

    1. As she takes us through the middle, Lahiri continues to balance two very different possibilities: separation and reunion.

    2. What can happen next? My advice is to make a habit of asking such questions.

C. The ending is where the conflicts exposed at the beginning—and explored through the middle—are finally worked out.

    1. Traditionally, plots resolved themselves in one of two ways: comically or tragically.

    2. Since the end of the 19th century, writers have been drawn to the idea of an open ending that may leave some questions unanswered.

    3. Lahiri's ending follows all of the rules laid down by Aristotle.

IV. Now we move on to the last two words of the five: "plot" and "story."

 A. These probably seem interchangeable, and in many situations, they are indeed used interchangeably.

 B. I would like to stick with the most famous definitions, established by the Russian formalists.

  1. "Plot" is the list of events in order of their presentation to the reader.

  2. "Story" is the same events listed in chronological order, the order of their original occurrence.

 C. How can this help us to get more out of our reading?

  1. It helps us to realize that events could have been presented to us in several different ways.

  2. So, if you are Lahiri working on "A Temporary Matter," you have to think not only about the death of the baby but about lots of other past events as well.

  3. Each of those past events needs to be placed or positioned for maximum effect.

V. How, as a reader, do you keep track of this stuff?

 A. On your first time through, maybe you cannot really notice all of these things. But that does not mean that your first reading is empty or useless.

 B. If you are really interested in such things—and do not mind rereading—you can go back and make a list of what happens in each section and list references to past events.

VI. Near the beginning of the *Poetics*, Aristotle says that we all delight in imitation.

 A. We learn our earliest lessons through imitation, he explains, and we take great pleasure in listening to stories and looking at pictures.

 B. All of this is natural, he believes. And so, he implies, is the wish to understand those stories—to take them apart and see how they were made.

 C. By now, it should be obvious that I agree with him completely. As we move into the middle of our course, I sincerely hope you are beginning to see why.

Suggested Reading:

Burroway and Stuckey-French, *Writing Fiction*, chap. 7.

Cobley, *Narrative*.

Questions to Consider:

1. What makes for a really good beginning? Are there any short stories or novels that have grabbed you right from the start? If so, what do those works have in common?

2. What makes for a good ending? It has been said that the ending is the hardest part of a story to get right. Do you agree? Can you think of works with strong beginnings, interesting middles—and weak or disappointing endings?

Lecture Eight—Transcript
Reading for the Plot—Five Simple Words

Hello, and welcome to Lecture Eight in our course on the "art of reading."

We're now almost a third of the way through the course, and we have covered a lot of ground. We've talked about authors, narrators, and characters.

We've learned that description is not an add-on, and that style should not be opposed to substance. Most recently, we've learned how to recognize even the most subtle uses of devices like irony and ambiguity.

That is a lot to cover. With each lecture I hope we've learned how to read more closely—and how to make reading more fun and rewarding.

One big issue has yet to receive much attention from us, however. I'm happy to say that we're now ready to deal with it in some detail.

What is that issue? Just think about it for a minute. We've done authors, narrators, characters, description, style, and irony. So what's left?

OK, I won't make you guess. It's the plot—the story, the arc, or shape or structure of the entire piece. It's beginning, middle, and end. It's what happens to the characters and what happens to us as a result.

It's all of that and more, I think. For plot is where almost everything comes together. Plot is what hooks us at the beginning—and keeps us reading through to the end. So we really do need to talk about plots—what goes into a plot, how plots can be arranged and presented, and a whole lot of other things, too.

Before we get started, I have to tell you—this is an enormous subject. Much has been said and written about it. Indeed, few subjects in the field of literary studies have ever attracted as much attention, or aroused as much curiosity, as plot.

In later lectures, we'll get into the finer points of plotting. When we look at novels like *Ivanhoe* and *Jane Eyre*, we'll touch on the use of subplots. When we reach the second half of the course, we'll talk about the construction of scenes and the alternation of scene and summary.

For now, however, I propose that we focus our attention on the essentials—the most crucial components of plot and plotting.

©2009 The Teaching Company.

Fair enough—but how should we proceed? I think we can make a very good start if we just remember five little words. Fortunately, we've already used three of them: "beginning," "middle," and "end."

So what are the others? "Plot" and "story."

Those words may not look like anything special. Two of them—story and plot—probably appear to be interchangeable. But just wait. By the end of this lecture, we'll see what the words mean, we'll find out where they come from, and we'll gain a better sense of what they can do for us.

In talking to students—and friends—about literature, I have noticed that although people are drawn to plots, they often find plots difficult to remember. People can recall particular scenes, but can't quite put those scenes in the right order. In other words, people don't quite see how the parts of a plot are related to the whole.

If people are lucky enough to remember the plot, they may, nevertheless, experience it as an almost random sequence of events: First this, then that, and then something else—just one darn thing after another. Here again, the problem is that the parts don't seem to be connected in any really meaningful ways. They haven't quite come together in the reader's mind.

I want your experience to be richer and more satisfying than that. I want you to look for larger patterns, to notice underlying shapes and overarching structures. That's why I'm making such a big deal of those five little words: "beginning," "middle," and "end," "plot" and "story."

To demonstrate their usefulness, I'll need to work with a really great example. As it happens, I have one in reserve. It's a short story called "A Temporary Matter." This story is the first piece in *The Interpreter of Maladies*, an award-winning collection by Jhumpa Lahiri. At first glance, this story might appear quite simple. The cast is small and the plot relatively straightforward. This is the story of two people, a young couple in their thirties. He's in grad school; she works in the city as a proofreader. It doesn't sound like much, does it?

Yet before we're three pages in, we see how much is at stake for this couple. For we're told that, six months prior to the start of the story, they lost a baby. He went away to an academic conference. She went into premature labor, and the child was born dead. It's hard to see how those stakes could be much higher.

In the work of fledgling writers, by the way, the stakes are seldom high enough. The characters don't seem to have all that much on the line—and as a result, we have little incentive to go on reading.

But here, as I say, the stakes are very, very high, indeed. For starters, we want to know how this couple will cope with their loss. Will it bring them together or drive them apart? If they do stay together, will they try for another baby?

Already, I'm guessing, you're curious. You want to know what happens. That's a clear sign that the writer knows what she's doing and where she's going.

With that in the background, let's get down to business. Let's begin in the most logical place—with beginning, middle, and end. Those words come to us from Aristotle's *Poetics*, a brief treatise largely focused on the art of tragedy. The *Poetics* is one of the earliest works of literary theory in the Western tradition, and it may still be the most important.

Much of the *Poetics* is devoted to the subject of plot. For Aristotle, plot is the central element in tragedy. At one point, he even goes so far as to say that plot is what a tragedy is "there for." You could have the actors come onstage and recite one great speech after another, he says, but that wouldn't add up to a plot—much less a tragedy.

Before getting into the business of beginning, middle, and end, Aristotle makes some very interesting points. Here are the most important ones.

Point number one: A plot is not unified simply because it relates the experiences of a single individual person. In writing the *Odyssey*, Aristotle explains, Homer did not include everything that ever happened to Odysseus. Instead, he was selective. He did some picking and choosing.

Point number two: In a good plot, a well-made plot, nothing can be eliminated—and nothing can be transposed or rearranged, either. So, if you find that you can eliminate a scene, or reorder a couple of scenes, you're dealing with a defective plot.

Both of those points might come in handy the next time you're at the movies. What if this scene were cut—or shifted to another part of the film? Would anyone ever notice the difference? If not, you may want to ask for your money back.

©2009 The Teaching Company.

That brings us to point number three: Each new event should happen because of—not just after, mind you—but because of the earlier events. In short, there should be a causal relationship among the events in the plot.

To illustrate this point, I'll borrow a wonderful example from E. M. Forster. That name may sound familiar, since Forster is responsible for the distinction between "round" and "flat" characters, which we discussed in Lecture Four.

Forster asks us to consider the difference between two very simple narratives. Here's the first: "The king died, and then the queen died." Got that? "The king died, and then the queen died."

OK, here's the second narrative: "The king died, and the queen died of grief." "The king died, and the queen died of grief."

According to Forster—and here he's being very Aristotlean—the first narrative is not really a plot at all. It's merely a series of events, one after another.

Why does the second narrative qualify as a plot? Because it connects the two events, identifying the first (the death of the king) as the cause of the second (the death of the queen).

Behind all of Aristotle's points, we can discover a disdain for "episodic plots." Those are plots in which scenes or episodes are not arranged so much as strung together. Remember what we said about "one darn thing after another"? That's what an episodic plot is like.

In moving from Aristotle's general rules to our particular example—the short story by Jhumpa Lahiri—we see that Lahiri's plot is by no means episodic. There are six sections in this story, and each of those sections—well, it's essential to the larger effect. If you eliminated any one of those sections, the entire structure would collapse.

What if you rearranged the sections, or shifted events from one section to another? Would that lead to a similar collapse? Maybe not—but it would change the entire mood and feeling of the story. To see what I mean, consider the death of the baby—which, as I noted earlier, is mentioned in the first few pages.

What if that event were shifted to some other part of the story? What if we didn't learn about the baby until the very end? That might make for a powerful conclusion, and I'm sure that any number of other writers might have chosen that approach.

Those writers would give us a "what's wrong?" story. They'd show us the sad young couple and make us guess at the reasons for their trouble.

Lahiri is going for something a little different. She also shows us the sad, young couple. Indeed, after letting us in on the death of their baby, she takes us back to the present, closing with a long paragraph on their growing estrangement.

But instead of encouraging us to ask "why?" or "what's wrong?" she makes us ask "what's next?" What can these people do to re-establish some emotional connection with each other? Is it too late for them, or will something happen to bring them back together again?

So, if you want a "what next?" story, instead of a "what's wrong?" story—and Lahiri does—you have to mention the baby's death sooner rather than later. If you move or shift it to another part of the story, you run the risk of making lots and lots of trouble for yourself.

This is the sort of thing that Aristotle helps us to see—and, really, not just to see, but appreciate and enjoy.

So far, so good. Now what does Aristotle have to say about beginning, middle, and end? How do those words, those ideas, figure into his argument?

To answer that question, we'll have to go beyond Aristotle—for although he insists on the importance of beginning, middle, and end, he doesn't spend much time discussing them.

I don't think it will be difficult to pick up where he leaves off. I just want to make it clear that what we're about to discuss, though inspired and informed by Aristotle, cannot be found in the *Poetics*.

OK, then. Beginnings. What are they, and how do they work?

At the beginning, we're introduced to the characters and their situation—which, at this point, is relatively stable. Problems may be lurking beneath the surface, yet for now they remain safely submerged. These problems are still manageable, bearable—and, in some cases, deniable. It's still possible to say that there isn't a problem, or that it isn't so bad, or that it will somehow take care of itself.

 ©2009 The Teaching Company.

But before long, that won't be nearly so easy. Before long, something will happen to expose or reveal the hidden problems and submerged conflicts. Once that event occurs, it will become increasingly difficult to deny the existence of the problem—increasingly difficult to live with it, too.

That event is sometimes called a "destabilizing event," since it knocks the characters off balance, preventing them from going on with life as usual. The destabilizing event can thus be said to set the entire plot in motion. It's like a jumpball, or a kickoff, or a faceoff. Before, everything is still and quiet—after, there can be lots and lots of action.

Is there a destabilizing event in Lahiri? I think so. In fact, I think that her beginning may feature two such events. Most obviously, there's the death of the baby. This event not only creates new problems—but throws old ones into sharper relief. It aggravates and exposes ongoing tensions between the partners in this marriage.

But before we find out about the baby, we learn about the arrival of a notice from the power company. The notice explains that the power will be shut off in the couple's apartment for an hour on each of the next five nights. All of this is explained, I should add, in the very first sentence of the story.

I know that doesn't sound like a big deal—the power company sends you these letters every day. But because it forces the couple out of their regular routine, the letter—the arrival of the letter—functions as another destabilizing event. For the next five days, these two people will have to eat dinner by candlelight. After dinner, he won't be able to work on his dissertation, and she won't be able to watch television.

This is a fantastic little bit of plotting: not one, but two destabilizing events pulling in opposite directions. The death of the child pulls the couple toward separation, while the power shutoff raises the possibility of renewed connection. If they can't work on the computer or watch TV, what will they do instead?

Though this is an impressive beginning, it's not entirely different from the beginning of most stories. Somewhere in the beginning, a period of relative stability is disturbed. The characters will be knocked off stride or forced out of hiding. They may even get into some trouble.

Once that has happened, we've come to the end of the beginning—or, if you prefer, the beginning of the middle.

As you might imagine, the middle is where complications arise. As we move through the middle, we get a better sense of what the characters are up against, and more often than not, we realize that things may get worse—and maybe a whole lot worse—before they get any better.

The middle section of Lahiri's story is no less impressive than the beginning. For as she takes us through the middle, Lahiri continues to balance two very different possibilities.

The first, as we noted earlier, is the possibility of separation. This couple has a whole lot of unfinished business to take care of. They need to talk about his depression—since the death of the baby he hasn't made any progress on his Ph.D. dissertation. They also need to talk about her increasingly obvious wish to avoid him.

Above all, though, they need to talk about the loss of the child. Does she blame him for its death? Does he blame himself? Does she want to try again? Does he? At this point, all of those questions remain unresolved—and yet, through the middle, Lahiri also encourages us to consider the possibility of reunion and reconciliation. The daily loss of power turns out to be a good thing—a very good thing. The couple seems to enjoy their dinners together. At her urging, they even begin to play a game sharing secrets—telling each other things they've never told before.

This is a "what next?" story, isn't it? It's a really, really good one, too.

So, what happens in the rest of the middle? Lots of things—you just have to read this one for yourself. But the most dramatic events are those associated with the secret-sharing game—for although this game brings them closer, it also seems a little risky, maybe even dangerous.

At first, the secrets are harmless and rather sweet. She sneaked a peek at his address book when they were dating. He forgot to leave a tip on one of their first dates.

Later, however, the secrets turn sour. He returned a sweater she gave him for Christmas and spent the rest of the afternoon drinking in a bar. She never really liked the one poem he managed to publish.

 ©2009 The Teaching Company.

Sweet and sour, comforting and dangerous—this is perfect stuff for the middle. Complications have definitely arisen. The characters need to make peace with each other—and with themselves as well. Clearly, they're testing each other. They're testing the strength of their bonds and commitments. What will happen next? What can happen next?

That's almost always a good question: What can happen next? So, my advice is to make a habit of asking such questions—in other words, don't just muddle through the middle.

One good exercise, I always think, is to imagine how these characters might be brought to a happy ending. Do the characters know what they want? If so, can they figure out how to get it? What obstacles do they face? What will it take for them to overcome those obstacles? Will it take a change of circumstances or a change of heart?

With all of that in mind, we're ready to talk about endings. The ending, well, that's where things get resolved. It's where the conflicts exposed at the beginning—and clarified and deepened through the middle—are finally worked out.

Traditionally, as you may know, plots resolved themselves in one of two ways. In a comic ending, you might witness scenes of reconciliation, marriage, birth, or rebirth. In a tragic ending, you would have to witness scenes of dissolution, exile, and death.

Since the end of the 19th century, writers have been drawn to the idea of an open ending. We saw this kind of thing in Chekhov—and again in Flannery O'Connor and Katherine Mansfield. An open ending may leave some questions unanswered. It may even leave the characters on the verge of some really important decision.

In case you're wondering, Lahiri's ending is devastating. As you know, I never like to spoil the ending, so let's just say that this one follows all of the rules laid down by Aristotle. It is tightly bound to both the beginning and the middle, and it's a natural outgrowth of earlier events in the past.

So there you have it: beginning, middle, and end.

Back at the beginning of the lecture, I told you that there were five little words in all, remember? We've covered three of them, and now we're moving on to the last two: plot and story. Those are the ones that probably seem interchangeable.

In many situations, they can be used interchangeably. Over dinner, in an e-mail to friends or family, even at a meeting of your book group, there's no reason to be all that picky: plot or story—story or plot. In those situations, it doesn't really make any difference.

In discussions among scholars, however, there is a need to be more precise—and that's where people tend to make sharp distinctions between story and plot. Unfortunately, scholars don't always use the words in the same way—and if you follow these debates closely, you may come away with the impression that each individual scholar has her own private definition of both plot and story.

This used to be a cause of some embarrassment to me, since it suggested that people in the field of literary studies, English teachers, couldn't agree on much of anything. I started to feel better when my friends in other fields—astrophysics, evolutionary biology—told me about debates within the scientific community over simple third-grade terminology. If scientists can't agree on the meanings of words like "planet" or "species"—and it's my understanding that they can't—then maybe it's OK if literary critics argue about story and plot.

Rather than covering the wide range of meanings assigned to these terms, I'd like to stick with the most famous definitions. These are the ones that spawned all the others, and they're the ones that my students generally seem to find most helpful.

I'm talking here about the definitions established by the Russian Formalists. The Russian Formalists were a loose confederation of theorists and critics. They lived and worked in Russia, and they did their most important research back in the 1920s.

Their names? Boris Eikhenbaum, Boris Tomashevsky—and my favorite, Viktor Shklovsky.

Several members of the group may have had a hand in the formation of the distinction between story and plot, but it seems to have been Shklovsky who first mentioned it in print. His remarks are a little cryptic, but not impossible to understand.

 ©2009 The Teaching Company.

Basically, he says the following: "The concept of plot is too often confused with a description of the events in the novel, with what I'd tentatively call the story line."

He then goes on to add that "the story line is nothing more than material for plot formation."

So, what can we take away from that? That the plot is more than just the events in the novel—it's more than just the story line— and that the plot has to be formed or shaped. It's made or produced—and so, perhaps, it might be made or produced in any number of different ways.

To flesh out these remarks and get a better sense of what Shklovsky is usually thought to mean by them, you'll need to engage in a little bit of imagination. It won't take long, and it will definitely pay off.

OK. First imagine making a list of all the events portrayed or mentioned in the course of a play, or a novel, or a movie—and I do mean all of them. If a character says something about his father's funeral or his brother's wedding—even if it happened a long time ago and even if it's only mentioned in passing—that event needs to go on your list.

Now imagine arranging the items on that list in two different ways. If you arrange them in the order of their presentation to the reader or the viewer, you get what we call the "plot." The first event on this list is the first one we see or hear about. The second one is the second one we see or hear about, and so on. Again, technically speaking, this is the plot.

So what about the story? The story is what you get if you arrange the very same events in their original chronological order. This time, the first event is the earliest event—the one that happened first. The second event is the one that happened next, and so on.

That probably bears repeating: So, plot is the list of events in the order of their presentation to the reader. Story is the same events, now listed in chronological order, the order of their original occurrence.

There's no reason why the two lists have to be different, by the way. There's certainly no rule against the exact alignment of plot and story.

When presenting these ideas in class, I usually ask my students to think of movies in which there's a striking difference between story and plot. It never takes long for some really great examples to emerge: *Citizen Kane*; *The Godfather, Part II*; *Pulp Fiction*. In each case, we get lots of flashbacks and flash-forwards, lots of gaps to fill, and lots of little mysteries to solve.

Indeed, much of the fun of watching these films consists of trying to derive the story from the plot—you follow me there?—trying to reconstruct the original chronology from the scattered bits and pieces available to us at any given moment.

There are also lots and lots of literary examples, and many of them will be featured in our upcoming lectures. In the Sherlock Holmes stories, in *Jane Eyre*, in *As I Lay Dying*—in all of those works—we're doing the same thing we do with a movie like *Citizen Kane* or *Pulp Fiction*. We're trying to reconstruct the original chain of events—trying to derive the story from the plot.

OK, so this happens a lot. But why is it such a big deal? How can it help us to get more out of our reading?

For one thing, it helps us to realize that events could have been "emplotted"—that is, presented to us—in several different ways. We've already touched on this issue in our discussion of Lahiri's opening. Remember when we talked about her decision to tell us about the death of the baby at the beginning of the story, instead of saving it for the end?

When you begin to think about emplotment in that way, you start to see that it actually requires many such decisions. For in addition to deciding how to begin and end, the author must figure out when and where to mention crucial bits of information from the past.

So, if you're Jhumpa Lahiri and you're working on "A Temporary Matter," you have to think not only about the death of the baby, but about lots of other past events as well: the couple's courtship, their life as newlyweds, their preparations for the arrival of the child. That's not all: There should also be references to their own childhood experiences and to their own parents.

Each of those things needs to be placed or positioned for maximum effect. In each case, you need to decide: Where should I put this?

 ©2009 The Teaching Company.

Where does it belong? Does it work better in the first few pages, somewhere in the middle, or closer to the end?

See how amazing that is? So many decisions to make—so much care and intelligence to exercise. To me, there's just no doubt that ideas of story and plot will deepen your admiration for a favorite author.

OK, then. We've said a bit about each of the five little words. Now, perhaps, only one question remains: How, as a reader, do you keep track of this stuff? Can you really notice all of these things on your first time through? On your first time through, maybe not—but that doesn't mean that your initial reading is useless. Even on the first reading, you can still make a point of looking for a destabilizing event. Read up to the first section break—or, in a longer work, the end of the first or second chapter—and see what, if anything, has happened to throw the characters off stride.

Then, as you read through the middle, try to keep track of the characters' stumblings and fumblings. Why can't they simply regain their balance? Are they in danger of falling flat on their faces?

If you're really interested in such things—and don't mind rereading—you can also go back and make a list of what happens in each section. You can also list references to events from the past. This is what I do whenever I'm getting ready to teach a story, make all of these lists—and I never, ever regret it.

Your lists should help you to reconstruct some of the decisions behind the arrangement or emplotment of the various events. Are events presented in more or less chronological order? If not—when, and where, and why do we jump back into the past?

My notes on the Lahiri story revealed one very interesting detail—a detail that I had not noticed on my original reading. In the first few sections of the story, details about the past are supplied by the narrator. She's the one who tells us about the death of the baby, for example.

In later sections, as the secret-sharing game gets underway, the characters take over this function themselves. They tell stories about the past—and they have to decide which stories to tell first and which to save for later.

My notes revealed, then, that this story not only provides a great example of emplotment, it turns out to be about emplotment. What stories do we tell, and when do we tell them? What do our stories mean to us, and what effects do they have on others? How can the messy, raw material of life be transformed into something like a story—something with a beginning, middle, and end.

Very cool.

Near the beginning of the *Poetics*, Aristotle says that we all delight in imitation. "We learn our earliest lessons through imitation," he explains, and we take great pleasure in listening to stories and looking at pictures.

All of this is natural, he believes, and so—he implies—is the wish to understand those stories, to take them apart and see how they were made.

By now, it should be obvious that I agree with him completely. As we move into the middle of our course, I sincerely hope you're beginning to see why.

Thanks as always for joining us. We'll look forward to seeing you soon.

©2009 The Teaching Company.

Lecture Nine
Master Plots—The Stranger and the Journey

Scope:

As we move into this lecture, our exploration of plot and plotting will take a somewhat fanciful turn. Instead of looking at the carefully crafted arguments of thinkers like Aristotle, we will consider a sweeping generalization attributed to any number of writers and teachers, that there are really only two master plots: "the hero takes a journey" and "a stranger comes to town." As we consider the implications of this claim, our first question will be the obvious one: Can it really be true? Are there really only two master plots? And if that is not true, what gives it the ring of truth? We may not succeed in identifying all of our examples with one of those two master plots, but we will have fun trying—and will learn more about narrative structures and readerly desires along the way.

Outline

I.   We extend our discussion of stories and plots by observing that the stories we like best are often very familiar.

  A.   Think about the Cinderella story, the rags-to-riches story, or the love-conquers-all story. These stories are sometimes called cultural myths, master narratives, or master plots.

  B.   We also need to consider the closely related issue of genre.

  C.   How can we learn to recognize master plots and genres?

II. We start with master plots.

  A.   Master plots are not exclusively literary.

  B.   Master plots are in many ways culturally specific.

    1.   There is often a historical dimension to all of this.

    2.   Master plots go in and out of fashion.

  C.   It is also possible to describe some master plots as more or less universal.

  D.   One version of this universalizing approach to master plots can be found in the advice of creative writing teachers— there are really only two basic stories or plots in all of human culture.

E. One thing to point out here: The enormous popularity of these two master plots attests to the importance of a destabilizing event somewhere in the beginning of the narrative.

III. Genre is the literary critical term for "kind," "type," or "category."

    A. We can also speak of generic distinctions when talking about other media and art forms.

    B. The most basic generic distinction in the literary world is the distinction between fiction and nonfiction.

        1. Nonfiction deals with the truth—it gives us the facts.

        2. Fiction, by contrast, puts us in touch with larger, often emotional, truths.

IV. At this stage in our discussion of genre, I need to make a couple of other points.

    A. First, as the terms "fiction" and "nonfiction" imply, genres are usually defined in opposition (or at least in distinction) to each other.

        1. Westerns are different from horror stories; legal thrillers are different from time-travel sagas.

        2. Some critics and scholars like to talk not only about particular genres but also about larger genre systems.

    B. My second point is that although the boundaries between genres are pretty well established, they are not always well policed.

V. Throughout this lecture, we have made passing references to various fictional genres, and in practice it is not very difficult to tell them apart.

    A. How do we know?

        1. The author's name may be a signal.

        2. Signals can also be sent by titles and cover art.

        3. What you are doing, as you process those signals, is assigning each of those books to a genre.

    B. One interesting thing to note here is that as writers have become more and more interested in crossing boundaries and mixing genres, publishers and booksellers seem to have grown more and more determined to use genres as marketing devices.

    C. More than those clues mentioned above, it is the opening sentences that help us to recognize the place of an unfamiliar work in the larger genre system.

©2009 The Teaching Company.

Suggested Reading:

Abbott, *The Cambridge Introduction to Narrative*.

Frow, *Genre*.

Questions to Consider:

1. Which of our two master plots ("stranger" or "journey") do you enjoy more? What are your favorite examples of each?

2. What sorts of characters, settings, and story lines would you expect to find in works with the following titles: *Objection Sustained*; *Saddle Up!*; *Dark Matter, Distant Planet*; *Death Takes a Sabbatical*; and *Return to Ravenwood*?

Lecture Nine—Transcript
Master Plots—The Stranger and the Journey

Hello, and welcome to Lecture Nine in our course on the "art of reading."

In our last lecture, we talked about stories and plots. We looked at beginnings, middles, and endings. We consulted Aristotle and the Russian Formalists.

We also saw how much goes into the organization of a plot: how many decisions the author has to make—how much care and intelligence goes into each one.

I'd like to extend our discussion of stories and plots. So, I'll begin this lecture by observing that the stories we like best—the ones we enjoy most—are often very, very familiar.

You know what I mean, don't you? Just think about the Cinderella story, the rags-to-riches story, or the love-conquers-all story. You've heard them all before—and yet, somehow, you never get tired of hearing them again, especially if they're told well.

These stories are sometimes called "cultural myths," or "master narratives," or—and this is the term that I like best—"master plots."

As we begin to think about master plots, a number of very interesting questions come into play: Why have these stories lasted so long? What is the source of their enduring appeal?

Are they "culturally specific"—that is, firmly rooted in particular histories and traditions? Or are they, instead, "universal"? Do they reflect the needs and concerns, the anxieties and fantasies, of all people at all times and places?

As we start to think about master plots, we'll also need to consider the closely related issue of "genre." As you probably know, "genre" is a term derived from the French word for "kind" or "type." A list of literary genres would include the mystery, the western, the thriller, the police procedural—to name but a few.

So, here we are: Lecture Nine, master plots and genres. How can we learn to recognize them? How do they shape our experience of reading? Is it really true, as some theorists have argued, that we can't begin to make sense of a book without placing it into a generic category? Short answer: Yeah, I have no doubt that that's true.

 ©2009 The Teaching Company.

Let's start, then, with master plots: recurring narratives or stories, the kind that seem—as I put it earlier—very, very familiar.

I've already mentioned a few examples—the Cinderella story, the rags-to-riches story—and you may have noticed some overlap between them. It may even be possible to argue that the Cinderella story is a version of the rags-to-riches story. In both cases, the central character rises from obscurity and poverty to wealth and fame. In both cases, his or her essential virtues are finally recognized and rewarded.

You may also have realized that these master plots are not exclusively literary. If so, you've made a really important discovery—for master plots not only figure into works of fiction, but also turn up in many, many other places: news articles, biographies, comic books, opera, movies. As theorist H. Porter Abbott has shown, they can even figure into political campaigns and murder trials.

These master plots are in many ways culturally specific. The rags-to-riches story reinforces the American belief in rugged individualism and self-sufficiency. It shores up our most basic values and aspirations. Yet, at the same time, we might also wonder about our attachment to the story—our need to hear it repeated over and over again. If you were really convinced that you could make it on your own, you wouldn't need so much reassurance that you can make it on your own.

There is often a historical dimension to all of this. Master plots go in and out of fashion, and it's fun to try and figure out why. So when did rags-to-riches stories first become popular with American readers? Were these stories around in the Colonial Period? Why did they make such a big splash in the second half of the 19th century? Why did the novels of Horatio Alger—the writer most closely associated with this particular master plot—begin to go out of print in the 1930s?

Once you begin to ask such questions, you've made an important step in your development as a reader. I make this point—and I want to stress it—because students often assume that the purpose of literary study is to compare or debate interpretations of individual works. Should we admire "the great Gatsby"? Or should we see him as a fraud?

I don't blame them for that. Students have had these debates in high school, and they have every reason to expect that they'll have the same debates again in college (and maybe in grad school, too).

In truth, though, that sort of debating is only part of what we do in my field. For in addition to talking about individual works, we look at cultural practices and historical trends. From time to time, as I hope you've noticed, I'm trying to give you a friendly little push in that direction. I think it'll add to your enjoyment of reading as well as your appreciation of literature.

OK, then. We've begun to talk about master plots—and we've also begun to see why they might appear to be culturally specific artifacts, rooted in the history of particular times and places.

Yet, as you may recall, this is not the only way of accounting for their remarkable staying power. It's also possible, as I suggested earlier, to describe some master plots as more or less universal—as stories with meaning and relevance for nearly all times and places.

So, maybe the rags-to-riches story is not simply an American story. Come to think of it, the British have their own versions of it—you might just remember Dick Wittington and his cat—and so, probably, do the French, and the Germans, and the Russians; not to mention the Chinese, Japanese, and Koreans.

If that's true, then maybe something like a belief in self-sufficiency and a need or wish for independence is common to almost all people. Maybe it turns up in all places and all times.

One version of this second "universalizing" approach to master plots can be found in the advice of countless creative writing teachers. These teachers know that their students have trouble with plots— plotting is often said to be the hardest thing for a young writer to learn—and so they assure their students that there are really only two basic stories or plots in all of human culture.

These are the real master plots, then. They're bigger and even more powerful than rags to riches or love conquers all.

So what's the first one? "A stranger comes to town."

And the second? "The hero takes a journey."

Got that? "Stranger comes to town." "Hero takes a journey."

©2009 The Teaching Company.

Examples? For "stranger comes to town," you couldn't do better than *The Cat in the Hat*. Just think about it: Two little kids are home alone. Suddenly, there's a knock at the door—and their lives are turned upside down.

What about "hero takes a journey"? There are lots and lots of fairy tales that work that way: "Hansel and Gretel," "Red Riding Hood," "Goldilocks." The Harry Potter stories are kind of like this, since Harry ventures from a temporary home with his Muggle relations to Hogwarts School.

Prefer a more distinguished version of "hero takes a journey"? Then try The Odyssey, Don Quixote, Tom Jones, David Copperfield, Jane Eyre, Tess of the d'Urbervilles—and don't forget The Lord of the Rings.

Are there any more recent examples? Absolutely—there's The Road by Cormac McCarthy. The title of that book pretty much gives it away, don't you think?

One thing to point out here: The enormous popularity of these two master plots attests to the importance of a destabilizing event somewhere in the beginning of the narrative.

Remember what we said about destabilizing events in Lecture Eight? Think about how it works in these cases.

First, "stranger comes to town": The stranger's arrival throws everyone off balance. Indeed, his arrival may lead to a renegotiation of all existing social relationships. What does the stranger want from us? Is it safe to be friends with him? If we do befriend him, can we still be friends with each other?

Same way with "hero takes a journey": Home may be nasty—as it is for Jane Eyre and Harry Potter—but at least it's not unfamiliar. You know what to expect, and you're pretty sure you can handle it. If you leave home, you'll be moving out of your "comfort zone"—and before long, you may find yourself in trouble.

After thinking about these master plots and looking at all of these examples, it really does begin to seem as if those writing teachers are on to something. Maybe almost all stories can be fit into one of these two categories. Maybe they are variations on "stranger comes to town" or "hero takes a journey."

If you're willing to consider that possibility, you may also be ready to look for examples of your own, and don't be afraid to turn the search into a game.

How would that work? Tell your friends and family about the master plots of the "stranger" and the "journey." See if they can come up with any examples you haven't thought of. Then, the next time you're meeting with your book club, wait for a lull in the conversation and ask, casually: "So, stranger or journey?"

This game is a lot of fun. It doesn't take long to get good at it, and it can teach you a lot—and I mean a whole lot—about narrative structures.

For example, you'll start to see how basic patterns can be varied. Maybe this time the "town" is an elementary school classroom, and the "stranger" a new substitute teacher. Or maybe the "town" is a family, and the "stranger" a new son- or daughter-in-law. Or—just one last example—maybe it's an English department trying to make room for a new colleague.

As for the "journey," well there are many, many variations on that one. Joseph Campbell, the great student of mythology, was interested in two variations: the "vision quest," in which the hero seeks a vision of what to do, or fight for, or believe in; and the "father quest," in which the hero leaves home to find his origins—and with them, his identity.

In the three original *Star Wars* movies—the ones from the 1970s and '80s—the journey of Luke Skywalker effectively combines both of these variations. Luke finds something to believe in and fight for— and he finds his father (his sister, too—but somehow that's not such a big deal). When you put these details together, you probably won't be shocked to learn that Campbell's work on mythology—on master plots, in other words—was an enormous influence on filmmaker George Lucas.

I must tell you, though, that when I'm playing this game, I usually need to see some sort of literal journey—in addition to the spiritual questing, I mean—before I'm ready to pull the trigger on "hero takes a journey." Getting rid of the literal journey makes it all a bit too easy—and takes the fun and the challenge out of the game for me.

 ©2009 The Teaching Company.

But don't let me tell you what to do—or how to play the game. As far as I'm concerned, you can make up your own rules. No matter which way you go, the experience of the game will sharpen your ability to identify basic patterns and appreciate clever variations.

At this point, it's probably time for a brief recap. We've talked about master plots, and we've also talked about two different ways of looking at them.

The first way is to see master plots as culturally specific narratives—with greater resonance in some times and places than in others.

The second way is to see them as more or less universal. Here our examples included "stranger comes to town" and "hero takes a journey."

Moving forward, our first point might be that these two ways of looking at master plots need not be mutually exclusive. You can say that although a few of these patterns appear to be universal—or nearly so—some others have special importance for particular groups of people living at particular times and in particular places.

Our next point might be that there are other ways of classifying or categorizing plots. In making this point, we'll move from our initial discussion of master plots into an examination of genres.

You'll remember that "genre" is the literary critical term for "kind," or "type," or "category." We can also speak of "generic distinctions" when talking about other art forms. In painting, for example, you've got still life, landscape, portraiture, and history painting—each with its own separate traditions and conventions.

The most basic generic distinction in the literary world—the one that helps to organize almost all of our bookstores and libraries—is, of course, the distinction between fiction and nonfiction. So, let's start there.

The basis for that distinction probably seems obvious: Nonfiction deals with the truth—it gives us the facts—and so it includes everything from biography and history or current events to books on gardening, investing, and dog training.

Fiction, by contrast, gives us … now how do we want to finish that sentence? If we say that fiction gives us lies, we'll make a nice, sharp contrast with the truth of nonfiction. But we'll also run the risk of putting fiction down, of associating it with fantasy and unreality—and somehow that just doesn't seem right.

For although fiction presents us with made-up stories and make-believe characters, it also puts us in touch with larger truths—the kind that don't always get into histories or biographies. These truths are often emotional truths—but not always. Works of fiction can provoke thought as well as feeling.

At its best, fiction provokes thinking about feeling. It leads us to an emotional reaction—then turns that reaction into the object of intellectual reflection. Why did that story stir up those feelings in me? Were my feelings appropriate? Were they intelligent? In other words, how has this story exposed me to myself?

Don't get me wrong here. Great journalists, historians, and biographers can also lead us to ask such questions—there's really no doubt of that. But what we need to realize here is that this dialectical experience—read, then feel, then think, then read some more—seems to be built into almost any encounter with fiction. I sometimes think that this experience is what fiction is for—that fiction does this for us and to us in a way that almost nothing else can.

At this stage in our discussion of genre, I need to make a couple of other points. First, as the terms "fiction" and "nonfiction" imply, genres are usually defined in opposition—or at least in distinction—to each other. Westerns are different from horror stories. Legal thrillers are different from time-travel sagas, and so on.

That's why some critics and scholars like to talk not only about particular genres, but also about larger "genre systems." They're trying to remind us that we can't really pull out a single genre and consider it apart from all the others.

My second point is that although the boundaries between genres are pretty well-established, they aren't always well-policed. Lots of works mix or blend genres to very good effect. Indeed, this sort of mixing seems more and more common.

We touched on this possibility briefly in Lecture Four—when I shared my wife's observation about mystery writer P. D. James. Remember? My wife said that some of the best popular writers take a form that's not character-driven (like the mystery) and give the characters a little more weight and shading.

 ©2009 The Teaching Company.

Another example of generic mixing might be the work of Philip K. Dick. His books are usually shelved with science fiction, but many of them draw on other forms, including the detective story. The most famous case is *Do Androids Dream of Electric Sheep?*—which became the basis for the movie *Blade Runner*.

What about something like *In Cold Blood* by Truman Capote? In that book, we cross the ultimate boundary—the one separating fact from fiction—and end up with a new form, which has sometimes been called the "nonfiction novel."

Capote was not the only writer to try this sort of experiment, by the way. In the 1970s, Norman Mailer based a book called *The Executioner's Song* on the life of Gary Gilmore—the first American to be executed after the reinstatement of capital punishment in the U.S. When Mailer died, many agreed that this was his most impressive work. It's long—and very, very dark—but well worth reading, especially if you're interested in generic mixing and blending.

Throughout this lecture, we've made passing references to various literary genres: the western and the horror story, the legal thriller and the time-travel saga, science fiction and hardboiled detective fiction, and so on.

My guess is that, in practice, it isn't very difficult to tell these things apart. Even if a number of books are mixed up at the front of the library or the bookstore—spread out on a table of new arrivals—we know immediately that this one is a mystery, that one a thriller, and that one a family saga.

How do we know these things? That is an interesting question. The author's name may be a signal. Even if you've never read Steven King or John Grisham, you know what to expect from them. Their names function almost like brand names in the supermarket: If you buy the King, you'll get something scary. If you go with the Grisham, it'll be something with lawyers—which may, of course, be scary in a different way.

Signals can also be sent by titles and cover art. If you look at the front of a book and see a gavel—and not, say, a rabid dog—chances are good that you're dealing with something more like *The Firm* or *The Client* than *Cujo*.

What you're doing, as you process these signals, is assigning each of those books to a genre. With those assignments come a whole bunch of assumptions—assumptions about what kinds of characters, plotlines, and themes the book is likely to include. As I say, all of this happens almost instantaneously—often in a matter of microseconds.

One interesting thing to note here is that as writers have become more and more interested in crossing boundaries and mixing genres, publishers and booksellers seem to have grown more and more determined to use genres as marketing devices. They realize, perhaps, that books require substantial investments of time from their readers—and so they want to make sure that readers don't often feel disappointed or misled.

Perhaps that's one reason why most trade paperbacks now include so many excerpts from reviews. You can usually find some excerpts on the back cover and a bunch more on the first few pages.

It may also help to explain why publishers solicit so many endorsements or "blurbs" from famous authors. These blurbs serve as recommendations, certifying the quality of the work within—they're a little like the old "Good Housekeeping Seal of Approval" in that way.

But that's not all they do. For blurbs also reinforce our assumptions about genre, working to crystallize our expectations of the characters and the plot. If you see a blurb from a writer famous for his whodunits, you can be pretty sure that this new writer also specializes in mysteries.

But more than anything else—more than the author's name or the title, the cover art or the blurbs—it's the opening sentences that help us to recognize the place of an unfamiliar work in the larger genre system. External signs may be useful, but internal evidence— evidence from the pages of the book itself—is often decisive.

To show you how this sort of evidence shapes our experience as readers, I'll ask you to join me in a new game. This time, I'll read the opening sentence of a novel—one we haven't discussed before—and ask you to make an initial guess about genre.

I could start you out with an easy one: "In a hole in the ground there lived a hobbit." That's from *The Hobbit* by J. R. R. Tolkein. Or maybe something like this: "A sharp clip-clop of iron-shod hoofs deadened and died away, and clouds of yellow dust drifted from over

©2009 The Teaching Company.

the cottonwoods out over the sage." That's *Riders of the Purple Sage* by Zane Grey.

By now, however, you're probably ready for something a bit more challenging. So, let's try this one: "The family of Dashwood had long been settled in Sussex."

Got that? "The family of Dashwood had long been settled in Sussex."

OK, then. What's your guess about the genre of that one? It doesn't sound much like Steven King or John Grisham, does it? It probably doesn't sound like Tolkein or Zane Grey, either—yet there are some pretty obvious clues here. The setting—the county of Sussex, in England—is not exotic. It's actually a rather ordinary place. The name of the family seems fairly ordinary, too.

A good guess would be that this is some sort of realistic novel. We won't see any great heroes here—no one like Achilles or Hector; no one like Hamlet or Macbeth, either. Instead, we'll see Mr. Dashwood, Mrs. Dashwood, and (presumably) a bunch of little Dashwoods.

In making such a guess, we might start to ask a few questions. How did the Dashwoods end up in Sussex? What social position or positions have they occupied there? Are they well-liked or well-respected? On their way up or on their way down?

These questions might extend to the plotline of the novel itself. Will the plot turn on conflicts between the family and its neighbors—or will it focus on conflicts within the family itself? What is suggested or foreshadowed by the phrase "long [been] settled"? Is the family about to be unsettled in some way? Will the destabilizing event be their departure from Sussex?

If any of these questions has occurred to you, then you are definitely on the right track because this, my friends, is the opening of *Sense and Sensibility* by Jane Austen. This novel is, indeed, the story of a family displaced from its ancestral home.

I'd like to play another round of this little game—I think we have time for one more—but before we begin, I want to make a larger point. For it seems to me worth noting that our guesses about genre are not only immediate and instantaneous—but inevitable. It's hard to keep yourself out of this particular guessing game. Indeed, it seems to me as if you have no choice but to get drawn into it.

So why is that? What do these guesses do for us?

It seems to me that they serve a couple of important functions. First, as we've already noted, they shape our expectations of a work. They help us to make predictions and establish tentative hypotheses. Second, and perhaps even more interestingly, they can also figure into our final assessments of a work.

Let's say, for example, that much of what you find in a book confirms your suspicions. You thought it would be a mystery—and indeed, it is. But let's add a further stipulation: Let's say that some of what you find is a little surprising. You wouldn't have expected to find much humor in this sort of book, and yet there it is. Or you might not have thought the characters would be particularly well-developed—and yet, however improbably, they are.

This sort of surprise is almost always pleasant, and it tends to enhance your enjoyment and appreciation of a book. It deepens your admiration for the author, too. For although we may like authors who live up to our expectations, we become attached to authors who try to exceed them. These authors approach the established conventions of a genre in the same way that a jazz soloist approaches a familiar tune: as the basis for something new and exciting.

Sometimes authors announce their departure from established norms right away—as Kafka does in the opening sentence of *The Metamorphosis*: "When Gregor Samsa awoke one morning from troubled dreams, he found himself transformed … into a monstrous insect." At first, that sentence appears rather ordinary—by the end, however, it seems anything but. From this point on, we know that the work will play with our expectations and confound our assumptions.

Lots of later writers have learned from Kafka. I often wonder if Gabriel Garcia Marquez isn't going for the same effect when, in the opening sentence of *One Hundred Years of Solitude*, his narrator says the following: "Many years later, as he faced the firing squad, Colonel Aureliano Buendia was to remember that distant afternoon when his father took him to discover ice."

In that case, the firing squad is bad enough—why is the colonel being executed?—and the discovery of ice is even worse. Since when does ice even need to be discovered? What kind of people have never seen it before?

 ©2009 The Teaching Company.

Of course, such announcements aren't always made in the opening pages. It sometimes takes quite a while to pick up on the signals—to discover clear, unambiguous signs of a book's departure from the norm. Either way, though, a certain kind of reader—dare we say, an artful reader?—will be up for this sort of challenge. Indeed, she'll not only welcome but embrace the challenge—and she'll see the fun in it, too.

OK, then. One more opening sentence before we call it quits.

Here goes: "Mr. and Mrs. Dursley, of number four, Privet Drive, were proud to say that they were perfectly normal, thank you very much."

That's Harry Potter again, right? So this round is over pretty quickly. But before we wrap things up, I'd just have you notice a few things. This sentence doesn't mention wizards, or quidditch, or any sort of magical anything. So, if you didn't recognize the source, you wouldn't necessarily know you were heading into a work of fantasy.

Yet, despite the absence of more obvious cues, there are some hints here. Look at the use of the word "normal," as in "they were perfectly normal, thank you very much."

Doesn't the smugness of that phrase—the awful, dismissive tone of it—make you wish (and maybe even long) for something unusual, and magical, and abnormal?

At this point, then, we may not know what's coming—but we have gotten our hopes up. We have been invited to dream of worlds beyond "number four, Privet Drive."

That brings us to the end of this lecture. I hope you'll agree that we've accomplished a lot in the last 30 minutes. We've extended our discussion of plots and stories—and in the process, we've also learned about master plots and genres.

I also hope you'll be glad to know that our initial survey of the elements of fiction is now complete. Before moving on to the second half of our course, we'll need to attempt some sort of synthesis. So, in the next three lectures, we'll try to collect our thoughts and apply our new insights to a series of increasingly complicated examples. We'll start with some entries from *The Casebook of Sherlock Holmes*.

Thanks as always for joining us. We'll look forward to seeing you soon.

Lecture Ten
The Game Is Afoot—Sherlock Holmes

Scope:

In earlier lectures, we have examined the basic elements of fiction. As we move through the next three lectures, we will apply our new insights to a series of increasingly complex examples. Our first examples will come from the casebook of Sherlock Holmes. Working with a number of Holmes stories—including "A Scandal in Bohemia," where the great detective is bested by a woman—we will confront some closely related questions: Why are the stories almost always told by Dr. Watson, rather than by Holmes himself? What psychological theories seem to underlie and organize the presentation of these characters? Why do these highly formulaic stories never seem repetitious or boring? And what, most importantly, can the stories tell us about the acts of reading and writing? The character of Holmes has often been described as both a reader and a kind of writer, and it is not hard to see why. He begins his detective work by examining and interpreting the clues left behind by his adversaries, and he almost always ends it by reconstructing the story of the original crime. It may be, then, that these stories are not merely great whodunits but little allegories of reading, demonstrations of how the intelligent reader trains his eye and engages his imagination.

Outline

I. This lecture will attempt a synthesis of the elements of fiction.

II. We start with some of the most basic elements of fiction: the author and the implied author, the narrator, and the characters themselves.

    A. The author and creator of Sherlock Holmes is Sir Arthur Conan Doyle.

        1. Doyle did not invent the detective story, but he should be recognized for his contribution to the development of serial fiction.

        2. Doyle's output was not limited to detective stories.

    B. What about the implied author?

        1. Doyle seems to have a bit in common with his famous detective.

 ©2009 The Teaching Company.

2. His politics are somewhat more obscure, largely because political matters seldom figure into the stories directly.

C. Now for the narrator: Only one of the Holmes stories is told in the third person; two are narrated by Holmes himself; and all the rest are narrated by John H. Watson, M.D.

    1. Watson is a thoroughly reliable narrator: the embodiment of common sense, decency, and domesticity.

    2. He serves as a counterbalance to the other characters and to Holmes himself.

    3. He also serves as a surrogate for the reader.

    4. The two stories narrated by Holmes are not very good, since Watson's absence is felt and Holmes often seems to be concealing something.

D. To examine the characters, we start with the issue of flatness and roundness.

    1. Watson's predictability—his flatness—is part of what makes him so endearing and is perhaps crucial to his effectiveness as the narrator.

    2. Holmes has a number of eccentricities and a dark side, but he never really surprises us.

III. The next item is description.

A. When Holmes's clients enter the scene, they are often described from head to toe. Holmes will use these descriptions to begin putting together the facts of the case.

B. As we read over the initial descriptions of Holmes's clients, we wonder which details will turn out to be most important.

IV. Next we review style, irony and ambiguity, plot, and genre.

A. The style is perfectly efficient. Doyle is not a minimalist, but rather his style moves us through the story as smoothly and efficiently as possible.

B. Doyle hardly ever makes use of verbal irony.

C. Plot: These stories are highly formulaic.

V. At this point, you may have some questions: How did the stories get to be so popular? Why do these plots deserve close attention?

A. Even the most rigid formula can leave some room for subtle variation.

B. Although in many ways predictable, the plots are not necessarily simple.

C. If we are going to follow the detectives, we have to begin in the middle and then make our way to the end—all while working to reconstruct events from the past.

D. As critics like Peter Brooks have noted, in almost any sort of detective story, the business of the plot is always the recreation of the story.

VI. Brooks takes us from plot and story to genre—and maybe beyond it, too.

    A. According to Brooks, almost every sort of story includes some reckoning with the past—some attempt to reconstruct or recreate what happened back then.

    B. All of this brings us back to the point that Sherlock Holmes is not only a reader but also a kind of writer.

Suggested Reading:

Brooks, *Reading for the Plot*, chap. 1.

Shklovsky, *Theory of Prose*, chap. 5.

Questions to Consider:

1. Would the stories be better if Watson were smarter? Would they be better if Watson were female? Imagine the following recastings of Dr. Watson and see what you think of each: Watson is an American or a Frenchman or a Russian; Watson is blind; Watson is a member of the royal family. (If you can think of others, feel free to consider them too!)

2. Doyle was responsible for popularizing the detective series, in which each episode presents us with a new puzzle to solve. Why does this form remain so popular? Do you see traces of the original Sherlock Holmes formula in recent detective, cop, or doctor shows?

Lecture Ten—Transcript
The Game Is Afoot—Sherlock Holmes

Hello, and welcome to Lecture Ten in our course on the "art of reading."

At the end of our last lecture, I promised that this one would attempt some kind of synthesis. While it's fun to look at the elements of fiction in isolation—and even more fun to consider their effects on our experience of reading—we shouldn't forget that these elements are supposed to come together in the end. They're supposed to add up to something larger and greater than the sum of their parts.

So how does that happen? How do characterization, and description, and plotting—to name just three elements—work together? Are these things always combined in the same ways? If not, how can we recognize and appreciate the differences?

These are big questions, and so I propose to make them the subject of our next three lectures. In those lectures, we'll move through a series of more and more complicated examples. We'll begin with the Sherlock Holmes stories, which almost everyone seems to know and love.

Then, in Lecture Eleven, we'll move on to *Ivanhoe* and *Jane Eyre*, to see how our ideas about reading can apply to much longer works. Then, in Lecture Twelve, we'll take up two very challenging works from the 20th century: *As I Lay Dying* by William Faulkner and *The Waves* by Virginia Woolf.

By the time we get to the end of this sequence, we should have a very good sense of how to draw on our knowledge of the various elements of fiction as we read works from a wide variety of periods and traditions.

For now, though, we'll have our hands full with Sherlock Holmes. So let's lay out an agenda for the rest of this lecture. The first order of business will be to see how various elements of fiction are treated in the Holmes stories. Why, for example, are the stories almost always narrated by Doctor Watson? What would happen if Holmes were the narrator? What would happen if we followed the criminals instead of the great detective and his sidekick? Why don't these highly formulaic stories ever seem repetitious or boring?

After working through these questions, we should be able to see why Holmes has so often been described as both a reader and a writer. He begins his detective work by interpreting the clues left behind by his adversaries, and he ends by exposing their foul intentions and spoiling their plans. So in order to do his job, the great detective has to be an expert at reading the evidence and telling stories. As a role model for artful readers, you could do a lot worse.

Let's start, then, with some of the most basic elements of fiction: the author and the implied author; the narrator; and the characters themselves. How do they figure into the adventures of Sherlock Holmes? The author and creator of Sherlock Holmes is Sir Arthur Conan Doyle. Doyle was born in 1859, attended medical school in the 1870s, and published his first short story in 1879. He was knighted in 1902, and he died in 1930. Since he's always presented as a Victorian, it's kind of surprising to learn that he spent so much of his life in the 20th century.

Two points need to be made about his literary career.

First, Doyle did not invent the detective story. Credit for that should go to Edgar Allan Poe. Poe's detective stories include "The Murders in the Rue Morgue" and "The Purloined Letter." They were published in the 1840s, several decades before the debut of Sherlock Holmes.

Interestingly, one of these stories is the basis for an early conversation between Holmes and Watson. You can find this in *A Study in Scarlet*, chapter 2. Watson says that Holmes reminds him of a character in Poe, and Holmes actually takes it as an insult, remarking that Poe's detective was "a very inferior fellow."

While Doyle is not responsible for the idea of the detective story, he should be recognized for his contribution to the development of serial fiction. Why? Because the Holmes stories were the first in which each new episode was more or less self-contained.

Let me take a moment to explain. Earlier forms of serial fiction were more like soap operas, with plot lines carrying over from installment to installment. But in the Holmes stories, each case would be wrapped up in 15 or 20 pages. By the time you got to the end, you'd know exactly who did it and why.

©2009 The Teaching Company.

Why is this worth noting? Because this was for many years a standard format on both radio and TV. Because it allows the author to enjoy the chief benefits of the soap opera—recurring characters, a sense of familiarity—without forcing the reader to keep up with every single installment, it remains pretty popular. When you think about it in that way, it's just brilliant.

The other chief point to make about Doyle's career is that his output was not limited to detective stories. He wrote lots and lots of other things, and there's reason to believe that he hoped to be remembered for them, rather than for Sherlock Holmes.

Indeed, as you may know, Doyle once tried to terminate the great detective. He made this attempt about 6 or 7 years into the series, in a story called "The Final Problem." Even if you've never read this one, you've probably heard about it. It's the story in which Holmes and his archenemy, the evil Professor Moriarty, fall to their deaths in a waterfall.

As you might expect, the public was upset. For about 10 years, Doyle stuck to his guns. But eventually, he bowed to public pressure and brought Holmes back into print. (You won't be surprised to learn that money was a factor in his decision.) After reviving the series, he published two more volumes of Sherlock Holmes stories, with the last volume appearing in 1927. By the end, the series included 56 stories and four complete novels in all.

One more point before moving on: Most people seem to agree that the best of the stories are the ones in the first two collections: *The Adventures of Sherlock Holmes* (which first appeared in 1892) and *The Memoirs of Sherlock Holmes* (from 1894). Almost all of the examples in this lecture come from stories in those first two collections.

If you enjoy those early stories—and I think you will—you might also want to read the two novels that preceded them: *A Study in Scarlet* (1887), where Holmes and Watson are introduced both to us and each other, and *The Sign of Four* (from 1890).

So much for the author—what about the implied author? What impressions of Doyle can we get or derive from the evidence of the stories themselves?

He seems to have a bit in common with his famous detective. He appears to be ruled by reason, not passion. The stories are always tightly organized. He's also well-read, displaying a broad knowledge of many different subjects.

Finally, he seems temperamentally conservative. He prefers order to chaos, and he likes it when things go back to normal. He recognizes the value of honesty and hard work, and he tends to punish characters who lie, and cheat, and steal.

His politics are somewhat more obscure, largely because political matters seldom figure into the stories directly. Doyle has been read as a critic of the establishment, but he also can be seen as a representative of the rising professional classes. Those two views of Doyle, they're not really incompatible, of course, since it's easy enough to feel that traditional elites should make way for those with expert knowledge and professional training.

So much for the author (the person whose biography we might read) and the implied author (the figure whose stories we know and love).

Next in line, then, is the narrator. Only one of the Holmes stories is told in the third person, and only two are narrated by Holmes himself. What about the rest? They are all narrated by John H. Watson, M. D.

So why should Watson be the narrator? What kind of narrator is he?

Let's take the second question first. Watson is a thoroughly reliable narrator. We never doubt his testimony—never suspect that he's embellishing the story. He tells us what we need to know—and seldom calls attention to himself in the process.

In many ways, Watson is the embodiment of common sense. He's not dimwitted, though he sometimes comes across that way in the movies. Indeed, he's got a medical degree from the University of London. He's also got a distinguished service record, having taken a bullet in the shoulder while serving in Afghanistan.

Watson also represents decency and domesticity. Though he and Holmes start out as flatmates, Watson eventually settles down, gets married, and moves out. Many of the stories begin with a kind of reunion between Watson and Holmes, with Watson returning to the old flat and getting drawn into his friend's most recent case.

©2009 The Teaching Company.

In short, Watson serves as a counterbalance to the other more-eccentric characters—and most obviously, to Holmes himself. More importantly, Watson also serves as a surrogate for the reader. Like us, he tries—and fails—to keep up with Holmes's deductions. Like us, instead of being embarrassed by that failure, he is delighted just to be in the presence of the great detective.

All of this helps us to understand why Watson is a perfect choice for the narrator. The narrator has to be capable of understanding and appreciating Holmes—he has to be able to follow Holmes's logic and grasp Holmes's conclusions. But he can't be so smart that he presents any sort of threat to Holmes—or, for that matter, to us readers. So what if we can't keep up with the master sleuth? Neither can anyone else, including his best friend!

Earlier, I told you that two of the stories were narrated by Holmes. They came very late in the series and may reflect Doyle's need for a change of pace. In any case, they aren't very good. Watson's absence is felt from start to finish. More importantly, Holmes often seems to be concealing something. We want to know when he first picked up on various clues—we want to follow along as he arrives at the solution—but our desires aren't satisfied until the very end, when he lays out his reasoning (as usual) in one fell swoop.

So, there's a pretty obvious question here: If you're Arthur Conan Doyle, and you're going to make Holmes the narrator, shouldn't you take advantage of the chance to let your readers share in the process of deduction? Otherwise, why dispense with Watson in the first place? Why not tell the story in the usual way?

Unfortunately, there is no answer to that question—at least not one that I can find. As I said before, Doyle simply seems to be going through the motions—looking for a way to create some sense of variety in a long-running series.

OK. Having talked about the author and the narrator, we're ready to examine the characters. Here, as before, we should try to apply some of the lessons learned in earlier lectures.

Let's start with the issue of flatness and roundness. You remember that E. M. Forster offered us an almost foolproof test for roundness: Is the character capable of "surprising in a convincing way"? If he never surprises us, he's flat. If he surprises but unconvincingly, he's flat pretending to be round.

OK, then. Does Watson pass the test? I'm afraid not. I can't claim to have read every single item in the Holmes "canon," but I can't remember a single time when Watson does or says anything surprising. Indeed, Watson's predictability—and perhaps, then, his flatness—is part of what makes him so endearing. It's also, as we've seen, crucial to his effectiveness as the narrator.

What about Holmes? Shouldn't he be able to pass Forster's test of roundness?

After all, he has a number of eccentricities. We're told, in the very first of the stories, *A Study in Scarlet*, that Holmes once beat a cadaver with a stick to see if bruises could be produced after death.

He has a dark side, too. In another early story, Watson says that Holmes has been "alternating … between cocaine and ambition." It's as if Holmes needs the drug as a kind of sedative. Without it, there's no telling what he might do.

In another early story, Watson says that Holmes has been "alternating from week to week between cocaine and ambition," so his habit is not a sometime thing. It's a kind of pattern that he falls into.

Later in the series, Holmes also admits that he has much in common with the criminals he investigates. Indeed, over the course of the series, he actually commits a few crimes. Mostly, it's small stuff—burglary, breaking and entering—but at least once, in "A Speckled Band," he might be held indirectly responsible for another man's death.

All of that stuff is great—yet, I'm still not sure that Holmes ever passes the Forster test of roundness. Maybe I'm just a tough grader, but I don't remember any time when Holmes really and truly surprises us. We may hear about his depression and drug use, but we almost never see them directly. It's the same way with his manic phases. He certainly gets excited from time to time, but he seldom loses control of himself or the situation.

What about the other characters? Most of them are flat as a pancake. They're usually driven by a single, simple motive. It may be vengeance, or greed, or fear, but whatever the case may be, they are seldom conflicted: They know what they want, and they go for it.

So, as intelligent readers, we may begin to sense that Doyle's understanding of human psychology is not especially complicated.

 ©2009 The Teaching Company.

Despite his interest in mysteries, he seems to regard the human personality as largely un-mysterious. If you know where and how to look, he suggests, you can figure out what other people are like—and what you'll find, in almost every case, is that they're a lot like you.

Holmes makes this point in a discussion with Watson: "You know my methods," he says. "I put myself in the man's place, and having first gauged his intelligence, I try to imagine how I should [myself] have proceeded under the same circumstances."

In other words: The other guy probably did what you would do; and so, if you want to figure out what he did, just put yourself in his place and ask yourself how you would have proceeded under the same circumstances.

At this point, you might be saying: "Well, great. But so what? Does our discussion of characterization in the Sherlock Holmes stories have any wider or broader application? Does it help us to think about other stories and other characters?"

Obviously, I think so. For one thing, I think it's good to be reminded of Forster's test for roundness, since that test is both easy and effective. It's also good to see that if a character fails the test, he may turn out to be endearing, or engaging, or effective in some other way.

It may seem natural and sensible to wish that Holmes and Watson were less flat and more round, but I'm not sure that the stories would really be better that way. In fact, it's quite possible that rounder, more complex characters would distract us from the main business of the plot—which is, of course, the solution of the mystery.

Finally, and this is a really important point, we need to unpack or uncover the psychological assumptions behind the treatment of particular characters. What is the book telling us about human behavior and human nature? The answer to that question is not really so hard to find, once you get in the habit of looking for it.

So, as in our earlier lectures, we see the importance of moving past initial responses ("I like this character" or "I can't stand that one") and attempting a more complex analysis. So let me ask you: Do you accept Doyle's account of human behavior? Do you agree that, when you get right down to it, people just aren't all that complicated—or that hard to figure out?

OK. So we're finished with authors, implied authors, narrators, and characters. The next item on our list is description—and this element could hardly be more crucial to the effect of the Sherlock Holmes stories.

If you've read any of the stories, you know that when Holmes's clients enter the scene, they are often described, again from head to toe. You also know that you have to pay very close attention to those descriptions, since Holmes will use them to begin putting together the facts of the case.

Examples? Too many to count. Take "A Case of Identity," an early story and perhaps one of the best. At the beginning of that one, Holmes and Watson look across the street and notice a woman wearing a fur boa, a broad-brimmed hat with a large red feather in it. The hat, just to complete the picture, is tilted in a "coquettish fashion" over the woman's ear.

After she has gone, Holmes asks Watson what he has gathered from the lady's appearance. Watson notes a couple of details, but draws only the most general conclusion—observing that she had "a general air of being fairly well to do."

Holmes says that although Watson has done "very well," he has "missed everything of importance."

"My first glance is always at a woman's sleeve," he explains. "In a man it is perhaps better first to take the knee of the trouser."

This delightful scene goes on for quite a while, with Holmes explaining that the sleeves of this woman revealed that she was a typist, rather than a sewing-machine operator. He then observes that her mismatched, half-unbuttoned boots made it "no great deduction to say that she came away [from home] in a hurry."

Remember how we said, a little while ago, that we join Watson in trying to keep up with Holmes? This scene helps to show how description figures into that process. As we read over the initial descriptions of Holmes's clients, we wonder which details will turn out to be the most important ones. Will it be the sleeves, the shoes, or something else? What should those details tell us about the client herself? What kind of life has she led? What kind of trouble has brought her to Sherlock Holmes?

 ©2009 The Teaching Company.

It may interest you to note that this sort of deduction was practiced by one of Doyle's teachers in medical school, who used it as the basis for his diagnoses of various ailments. Doyle often identified this man as the model for Sherlock Holmes and dedicated the first volume of Holmes stories to him.

So, what's left? In order: style, irony and ambiguity, plot and genre.

Let's begin with the topics that can be handled quickly, starting with style.

It's never less than perfectly efficient—exactly what you'd expect from someone like Doctor Watson. There are very few unfamiliar words and not many sentences that run for more than two or three lines.

So does that make Doyle some kind of minimalist? Not really. For unlike Hemingway, who often seems to be holding something back, Doyle and Watson appear to be telling us everything they know. Their aim is not to suggest the presence of emotional distress, but rather to move us through the story, to get us from page to page, as smoothly and efficiently as possible.

With that point in the background, it's no surprise to discover that Doyle hardly ever makes use of verbal irony. Minor characters may lie or stretch the truth, but that's not the same as being ironic—and in any case, our heroes Holmes and Watson, they always say exactly what they mean.

What's more, by the end of the story, any discrepancy between appearance and reality has disappeared—I mean, disappeared completely. There's nothing left of the original mystery. Holmes and Watson know everything there is to know—and so do we.

That leaves us with plot—at first glance that may appear to be another simple topic, for these stories are highly formulaic. They almost always follow the same pattern—and almost always unfold in exactly the same way.

The underlying pattern of the stories was first laid out by Viktor Shklovsky. (Remember him? He's my favorite Russian Formalist from Lecture Eight. Now do you remember?)

According to Shklovsky: "The general schema of Conan Doyle's stories is as follows: [Here I'm quoting from Shklovsky's groundbreaking essays on the stories, originally published in Russian almost 100 years ago.]

1. Anticipation, conversation concerning previous cases, analysis.
2. The appearance of the client. The business part of the story.
3. Clues introduced into the story.
4. Watson misinterprets these clues.
5. A trip to the site of the crime, which very frequently has not even been committed yet. By this device, the story attains narrative vigor.
6. The official detective offers a false resolution. If there is no official detective, then the false resolution is furnished by a newspaper, a victim, or by Sherlock Holmes himself.
7. The interval is filled in by the reflections of Watson, who has no idea what is going on.
8. The denouement is, for the most part, unexpected. For the denouement (and that's a fancy word for conclusion), Doyle makes frequent use of an attempted crime.
9. Analysis of the facts made by Sherlock Holmes."

There you have it! The most popular series of short stories in literary history—reduced to a simple formula. There's one other point that we need to make here. Point number 2 on Shklovsky's list, the appearance of the client, that's a classic destabilizing event, right? Holmes and Watson are sitting around. He's playing the violin; they're doing whatever—and then boom, the client shows up, and they're off to the races. Part of what we have to understand here is why, if these stories are so formulaic, they eventually became so popular?

For starters I'd say that even the most rigid formula can leave some room for subtle variation. I'd remind you that the presence of these variations—little departures from the norm—often gives us a great deal of pleasure.

Shklovsky hints at this fact when going through the items on his list. In discussing step 6, for example, he sees a couple of different possibilities. It all depends, he says, on the presence or absence of an "official detective"—usually a local constable. He enjoys the chance to catalog these variations—Shklovsky does, and so, I'd argue, do we.

Having made this point, I'd go on to say that although the adventures of Sherlock Holmes are in many ways predictable, their plots are not necessarily simple.

To explain myself, I'll ask you to play another round of the "what if" game. I trust you remember how this goes, right? What if Hawthorne had written like Poe? What if Lahiri had waited until the end to tell us about the death of the baby?

OK. This time, ask yourself what would happen if, instead of following Holmes and Watson, Doyle had followed the criminals, instead.

How would that work? In the first few pages, we'd see the criminal or criminals hatch their scheme. Later, we would see them try to cover their tracks. Finally, we'd see them slip up and get caught. Holmes could still figure into this arrangement, but he wouldn't enter the picture until halfway through.

Doyle's reasons for rejecting this arrangement are not hard to imagine. For one thing, it takes away all the mystery. We'd never be in doubt about what the criminals were up to. Indeed, we'd know all of their plans from the start.

More importantly, I think, we'd be deprived of any opportunity to match wits with Holmes. We'd be way ahead of him, in fact, and at times we might even begin to ask when he'd catch up with us. What fun would that be? No fun at all, if you ask me.

So, for the Sherlock Holmes adventures to work, events cannot be arranged in chronological order. If we're going to follow the detectives, we have to begin in the middle and then make our way to the end—all the while working to reconstruct events from the past.

In other words, these stories cannot achieve their desired effects without distinguishing—and here we're going to be technical—plot from story. For the business of the plot is nothing less than the successful re-creation or reconstruction of the original story. Indeed, the plot cannot end unless that reconstruction project is complete.

As critics like Peter Brooks have noted, this is true not only of Doyle's work—but of almost any sort of detective story. The business of the plot is always the re-creation of the story—always.

So, Brooks takes us from plot and story to genre—and maybe beyond it, too. According to Brooks, almost every sort of story includes some reckoning with the past—some attempt to reconstruct or re-create what happened back then. This reckoning is not unique to detective fiction, but it plays a more obvious role there. So, we may find a reason to elevate that apparently humble genre, the detective story, over all others—to see the detective story as something like "the narrative of all narratives."

All of this brings us back to a point that I mentioned at the very beginning of this lecture. This point is vitally important to Brooks, and I think it should be important to us as well.

What is the point? Simply, that Sherlock Holmes is not only a reader, an interpreter of clues and testimonies, but also a kind of writer. Given a bunch of bits and pieces, he must assemble a coherent narrative. What's more, as we've seen, his success depends on the use of imagination and the capacity for empathy. What is it he says to Watson? "I put myself in the man's place, and … try to imagine how I should myself have proceeded under the same circumstances."

It may be, then, that these stories remind us of the intimate connection between reading and writing. I say "remind" because I hope that this point is now familiar to you. At so many times along the way, we've imagined rewriting a story, or a paragraph, or a sentence. What effect would our revised version have on an artful reader? What responses would it be most likely to provoke? What might this little bit of rewriting or revising tell us about the intentions of the original author?

At this point, then, we may be ready to say that all readers are a little bit like Sherlock Holmes. All of us read and write at the same time—even if we never put pen or pencil to paper.

So much, then, for our first attempt at synthesis. I hope that we've begun to see how the elements of fiction can come together to make something special for the reader. I'm also hoping to expand that vision in our next lecture, when we turn to *Ivanhoe* and *Jane Eyre*.

Thanks as always for joining us. We'll look forward to seeing you soon.

   ©2009 The Teaching Company.

Lecture Eleven
The Plot Thickens—Scott and Brontë

Scope:

In this lecture, we turn our attention to longer and more challenging works of fiction, applying what we have learned about writing and reading to a pair of classic texts. In the first of these works, *Ivanhoe*, by Sir Walter Scott, the emphasis is on spectacle and action. The narrator describes his medieval settings and characters in rich, vivid detail. What is more, he organizes the story around a series of highly dramatic events: a jousting tournament, the siege of a castle, and the trial of one of his most appealing female characters. He does not, however, supply much in the way of emotional or psychological analysis. For a more complex investigation of human desire and a more complex plot, we turn to our second example, *Jane Eyre*, by Charlotte Brontë. The action in Brontë's novel, though always gripping, is almost always psychological. The real story here is Jane's development—emotional, moral, and spiritual—from childhood to maturity. So, although we are curious to know what Jane will do, our main concern is with her feelings: Will she ever fit in or find a place where she belongs? Will she find a partner who recognizes her many virtues? What does she really want out of life, and does she have the strength to get it?

Outline

I. Our agenda for this lecture is to take what we have learned about reading and test ourselves against really hefty books.

   A. Two such books are *Ivanhoe*, by Sir Walter Scott, and *Jane Eyre*, by Charlotte Brontë.

      1. Both of these works are at least 400 pages long and are classic British novels written in the 19th century.

      2. *Ivanhoe* is a historical novel set in the 12th century, and the emphasis is largely on spectacle and action.

      3. *Jane Eyre* is set in the 19th century, and the story is of Jane's move from the margins to the center, with the main focus on her feelings.

   B. The length of the work does make a difference.

      1. Short stories tend to focus on one or two characters; novels can include dozens of people.

2. A short story tends to focus on a limited period of time; a novel can span decades and take the main character from birth to death.
3. Short stories almost never include any subplots; novels offer multiplots.
4. Novels are like symphonies; stories are like chamber music.

C. How do these formal differences affect our reading experience?
1. A short story can, and probably should, be read in a single sitting.
2. Novel reading can stretch over days or weeks, and details might be forgotten.

D. How can you make reading a novel more like reading a short story?
1. Get in the habit of prereading.
2. Then dive into the opening chapters of the book.
3. Spend at least half an hour with the new book.
4. When you get 50 or 60 pages in, go back and reread the first 10 or 12 pages.

II. What might it be like to start reading a novel like *Ivanhoe* or *Jane Eyre*?

A. If you do some prereading of *Ivanhoe*, you will see that the book is divided into three parts, or volumes.

B. What else is revealed by a prereading of *Ivanhoe*?
1. The first volume of the novel is preceded by an announcement and a "dedicatory epistle."
2. We do not really need to bother with them, because they are often more trouble than they are worth.

III. After prereading *Ivanhoe*, you are ready to take on the first few chapters.

A. Here you will find a destabilizing event caused by a stranger that comes to town.

B. The novel begins by locating us in England, which is still reeling from the invasion of the Normans in 1066.

C. The narrator introduces a swineherd and a jester.

D. In the next chapter, we witness the arrival of 10 men—all of them new to these parts. Two of these travelers are a Cistercian monk and a Knight Templar.

©2009 The Teaching Company.

E. The beginning of *Ivanhoe* covers about five or six chapters where the two new strangers make their way to the home of Cedric the Saxon.

F. Through these chapters, we are also introduced to some other strangers: There is a pilgrim, and there is Isaac, a Jewish traveler. Here we have a good example of how subplots are introduced and developed.

IV. Do any of our old tricks work with *Jane Eyre*? Of course they do.

   A. As a result of our prereading, we know that the novel makes use of the three-part format.

   B. The novel begins with Brontë using our other major master plot: the hero takes a journey.

   C. The story is written in the first person, and we feel an immediate connection with this narrator and with the book itself. We are told about the setting, and we connect this description to the characterization of the unpleasantness of Jane's situation.

   D. What about her journey?
      1. It starts on that very first page, when we see that she will never find a secure, comfortable place with the Reeds.
      2. The journey begins in earnest, however, at the start of chapter 5 when Jane goes away to school.

   E. What can we make of all this?
      1. We can still find a simple, familiar structure in this novel: the hero takes a journey.
      2. Without knowing the ending, we can already identify Jane's journey as a quest for self-mastery, self-respect, and self-acceptance.

Suggested Reading:

Flint, "The Victorian Novel and Its Readers."

Tulloch, "Introduction."

Questions to Consider:

1. Which would strike you as the more impressive artistic achievement: an ambitious but flawed novel of 600 pages or a brilliant, virtually perfect story of 15 pages?

2. Would you rather read a novel published in the 19th century or one published last month? Whose recommendation would you be more likely to take seriously: that of a professor, that of a bookstore clerk, or that of a close friend?

Lecture Eleven—Transcript
The Plot Thickens—Scott and Brontë

Hello, and welcome to Lecture Eleven in our course on the "art of reading."

By now, you've probably noticed that almost all of our examples have been works of short fiction. In Lecture Three, we looked at tales by Poe and Hawthorne. In Lecture Four, we explored a short story by Chekhov. In Lecture Five, we did stories by John Updike and Flannery O'Connor, and so forth.

Most of these works are between 20 and 25 pages long. (That's also true of most Sherlock Holmes stories, by the way.) To be sure, we have made a few exceptions: *A Christmas Carol* (from Lecture Two), 90-pages long; *The Bear* (from Lecture Six), 132 pages; *The Great Gatsby* (also from Lecture Six)—that's a full-fledged novel, finishing at 180 pages.

It's fair to say, then, that we have yet to test ourselves against a really hefty novel.

So, our agenda for this lecture is to take what we've learned about reading and see how it might apply to big books. The lecture will deal with two such books: *Ivanhoe* by Sir Walter Scott and *Jane Eyre* by Charlotte Brontë.

Both of these works are at least 400 pages long—more than twice as long as *Gatsby*. Both are classic British novels, and both were written in the 19th century: *Ivanhoe* in 1819 and *Jane Eyre* in 1847.

That, however, is where the similarities end.

Ivanhoe is what we would call a historical novel, set in the 12th century. In this book, the emphasis is largely on spectacle and action. The story is organized around a series of highly dramatic events—a jousting tournament, the siege of a castle, and a trial—but there's not much in the way of emotional or psychological development. I don't think that any of these characters could pass the "roundness test."

By contrast, *Jane Eyre* is set in the 19th century. Politics does enter the novel, but in this case (as we used to say back in the 1980s) the personal is the political. Jane is an outcast, a marginal figure, who often protests against injustice. The real story is of her move from the margins to the center, and that story takes her from childhood to maturity. From start to finish, our main focus is on Jane's feelings: What does she really want out of life, and will she find the strength she'll need to get it?

So far, so good. But does the length of the work really make a difference? Is there any reason to think that reading a short story (or even a short novel like *Gatsby*) is different from reading a longer work like *Ivanhoe* or *Jane Eyre*?

I think so. In developing that point, I want to make a few general remarks about stories, novels, and the differences between them.

I'll start by noting that short stories tend to focus on one or two characters. You might think here of Gurov and Anna, the couple from "The Lady with the Dog"—or of the husband and wife from "A Temporary Affair."

By contrast, novels can include dozens and dozens of characters. My favorite edition of *War and Peace* includes a tightly packed list of more than 70 major characters.

Similarly, a short story tends to focus on a limited period of time: a day; a few weeks or months; maybe, if the author is really ambitious, a year or so. A novel—as I suggested in my little summary of *Jane Eyre*—well, that can span decades and take the main character from birth to death.

A more recent example would be *The World According to Garp* by John Irving. Irving's novel begins before Garp is born and ends with a chapter telling what happens to other characters after he dies.

Because its focus is relatively narrow, a short story almost never includes any subplots. We seldom shift our attention from one set of characters to another, as we do in novels like *Vanity Fair* or *War and Peace*. In that sort of "multiplot novel," the plot really does thicken.

To sum up, then: Novels are like symphonies, and some of them are like symphonies by Beethoven or Mahler. They can get big—really big. Short stories—more like chamber music: smaller; more intimate; less ambitious, perhaps—but more likely to achieve perfection.

Fair enough. But what does that mean to us as readers? How do these formal differences affect our reading experience?

To answer that one, let's start with an obvious but crucial point. A short story can—and probably should—be read in a single sitting. To get

 ©2009 The Teaching Company.

through 20 or 30 pages, you'll need half an hour—45 minutes, tops. So, the reading of a short story is a continuous, uninterrupted experience.

Reading a novel is nothing like that—especially if the novel was written in the 19th century. Novel reading can stretch over days, maybe even weeks—so it has to be mixed in with all kinds of other things: work; school; trips to the store, or the mall, or the doctor's office; walking the dog or cleaning up after the cat. You get the idea.

So, when reading a short story, there's not much chance you'll get lost in the middle or forget what happened in the beginning. If you are interrupted or do forget some important detail, it's not hard to go back and find it again.

When reading a novel, it's not so easy. Characters may drop out of the story for long stretches at a time. Or the story may shift from one set of characters to another—leaving you a little bewildered, uncertain of how to find your way back again.

So, how can you cope with such dangers? How can you make reading a novel more like reading a short story?

For starters, you might get in the habit of "prereading." Instead of just plunging into the book, leaf through it to see how the thing has been subdivided. Are there chapters? If so, are they of equal length? Are the chapters grouped together into parts, or volumes, or books? What might those subdivisions suggest about the larger shape or direction of the work as a whole?

In addition, make a habit of jotting down a few notes on a scratch pad. If the book is from your own library, you can also use the blank pages inside the front and back cover.

Don't go overboard with this. You're not going to be tested on any of it. Just make a list of major characters—and the pages on which they make their first appearances. Maybe add page numbers for favorite passages or scenes. This can be especially helpful if you're reading for a book club or class discussion.

When you finish your prereading and dive into the opening chapters of the book, try to make sure that your first encounter is a long and satisfying one. If you can, spend at least half an hour with the new book—enough time to get a sense of its style, its approach to characterization, and its handling of story and plot.

Later, when you get 50 or 60 pages in, go back and reread (or at least skim) the first 5 or 10 pages. They'll look different this time. Themes, conflicts, problems—all will be more obvious (and more interesting) on a second reading.

Whatever you do, don't worry. Because even though you're moving on to more challenging material, you can still make use of everything you've learned in our course. You can still think about authors, narrators, characters. You can still pay close attention to description, style, and the use of irony. You can still have a lot of fun with plot and genre.

In our last lecture, the one featuring Sherlock Holmes, we looked at those issues one by one. In this lecture, I'd like to be more creative— and more flexible. So instead of doing some sort of inventory of literary devices and techniques, let's see what it might be like to start reading a novel like *Ivanhoe* or *Jane Eyre*.

A little bit earlier, I said that it often makes sense to begin by trying to get a bird's eye view of the work—looking to see if and how it's subdivided.

If you do that sort of prereading with *Ivanhoe*, you'll see that the book is divided into three parts or "volumes." You may also notice that each volume includes 14 or 15 chapters—so already it seems as if balance and symmetry will be important aesthetic values here.

It also appears as if Scott may be working with an Aristotlean concept of plot structure: Three parts can't help but conjure an image of beginning, middle, and end.

In working through these possibilities, I should probably offer a historical footnote. During Scott's lifetime, a work like *Ivanhoe* was not published as a single, standalone volume—instead, it appeared as a three-volume set.

Why was this? At the time, most readers didn't buy books—they borrowed them from circulating libraries, which are a little bit like video stores. This way of publishing the book made it possible for three readers to be working on the same work at the same time.

This arrangement was actually developed by and for Scott, and it became enormously popular with 19th-century publishers and readers. The resulting product was known as a "triple-decker," and it should come as no surprise that *Jane Eyre* was first published as a triple-decker as well. Like *Ivanhoe*, in other words, it is subdivided into three equal parts.

Since the demise of the triple-decker at the end of the 19th century, lots of other schemes and subdivisions have been tried.

For example, William Faulkner divides *The Sound and the Fury* into four parts. Each part is dated, rather than titled, and if you write down the dates you'll see that they're not in chronological order. If you were to read the sections in chronological order, you might be less confused—but you would also destroy the structure and effect of the original novel.

John Updike divides *Rabbit is Rich* into five parts, which may remind you of one traditional structure for a play. Shakespeare's earliest editors divided his plays into five acts, for example. Looking at Updike's novel, you might also notice that the parts are unequal: The first four parts are all about 100 pages long, but the fifth is much shorter—only about 35 pages in all.

One final example: *Beloved* by Toni Morrison. This novel is divided into three parts, which suggests that it's going for something like that old triple-decker effect. But that suggestion goes out the window when you count up the pages, since the first part is over twice as long as the second, and the second part is about twice as long as the third.

In case you're wondering, *The Sound and the Fury* comes from the 1920s, while *Rabbit* and *Beloved* both come from the 1980s.

All of that is interesting, but how does it help us? How does it figure into our reading experience?

In responding to this question, I'd liken the sort of exercise we're doing to the quick aerobic warmup you might do before lifting weights or playing racquetball. I've made this analogy before, I know, but I think it's a good one. Before you can get in "the zone," you need to get limbered up, get the blood pumping—at least I do.

I also believe that you're more likely to enjoy a book—to appreciate it deeply—if you begin with some idea of where it's going. If you assume that Updike is simply moving from page 1 to page 437, you enter the book with one set of expectations. You expect a series of events—one thing after another—instead of a shapely, well-organized plot.

But if you know that Updike will be stopping and starting five times, you might expect something a little different. You might even begin to see each section as an aesthetic object in its own right—a little like the movements in a symphony—and you might find yourself asking a number of interesting questions: Will each section have a different feel or a distinctive shape? How will each section begin—and end? Will we see any cliffhanger endings, or will the sections conclude more neatly and gracefully? That's not all—because even as you begin to think about the individual parts, you'll probably also begin to wonder how the parts will come together in the end. After all, a great symphony is more than a series of beautiful movements—it's a total emotional experience, one with a powerful sense of coherence, and wholeness, and unity.

That's also true of a really good book. The chapters, or sections, or volumes—it doesn't really matter what they're called—are all, finally, part of a larger structure. The best way to get a feeling for that structure, I've found, is by prereading.

What else is revealed by a prereading of *Ivanhoe*? For one thing, a preread shows that the first volume of the novel is preceded by two shorter texts: an announcement or "advertisement" from "the author of *Waverley*"; and a "dedicatory epistle" or letter to "the Rev. Dr. Dryasdust" from someone called "Laurence Templeton."

What are these things doing here? Who are Templeton and Dryasdust? What about the author of *Waverley*? Do we really need to bother with any of this stuff?

My answer may surprise you—because this time it's "no." I don't think you need to worry about the advertisement or the epistle. It's not unusual to find such things in a work from this period—and they're often more trouble than they're worth.

OK, OK—but who is Templeton? It wouldn't hurt to know, right? Technically, he's the narrator of *Ivanhoe*. He's also a kind of screen or surrogate for Sir Walter Scott, who published his novels anonymously.

What about the advertisement? Actually that comes before the epistle—it's the very first thing in the book—and it assures the reader that, despite the presence of Mr. Templeton as narrator, *Ivanhoe* was actually written by the author of *Waverley*.

 ©2009 The Teaching Company.

Waverley was Scott's first novel, and because it made such a big splash, he continued to use it as a kind of brand name. The idea is not unfamiliar to us today: "If you liked *Waverley*, you'll just love *Ivanhoe*!"

I mention all of this because classic novels are often surrounded by dedications, forewords, and prefaces. *Jane Eyre* includes both a dedication and a preface, as well as a note to the third edition. These materials can be off-putting and tedious—we might as well admit it—and I'd hate to see you get bogged down with them.

Once you're finished with your prereading of *Ivanhoe* and you've gotten some sense of how the book is laid out, you're ready to take on the first few chapters. What will you find there? Do those chapters include any of the things we've learned to expect from the beginning of a short story? Is there a "destabilizing event"? What about a "stranger" or a "journey"?

Fortunately, the answers to these questions emerge quickly. Yes, there is a destabilizing event—and yes, a stranger does come to town.

The novel begins by locating us in time and space. This is "merry England," near the end of the reign of Richard I—that's Richard the Lion-Hearted. At this time, England is still reeling from the invasion of the Normans in 1066. As the narrator puts it:

> Four generations had not sufficed to blend the hostile blood of the Normans and Anglo-Saxons, or to unite, by a common language and mutual interests, two hostile races, one of which still felt the elation of triumph, while the other groaned under all the consequences of defeat.

So we need to revise what we were saying before. This time, it's not just one stranger—it's a whole bunch of them. It's the Norman Conquest. They showed up uninvited and basically took over the place—and things have never been the same since. Talk about a destabilizing event!

Having painted the historical backdrop, the narrator places us in a "rich glassy glade" and introduces the first two characters: a swineherd and a jester or fool. Both characters are described from head to toe, in keeping with Scott's usual practice—a practice familiar to us from Lecture Three. From the start it's clear that these characters are at home in this place—in other words, they're locals, not strangers.

They're also Saxons—and so they are members of the group that's been "groaning under all the consequences of defeat." Their world has been destabilized by the arrival of the Normans—and unfortunately, it's about to be upset again.

How do we know that? In the next chapter, we witness the arrival of 10 men—all of them new to these parts. Two of these travelers are singled out for special attention. The first is quickly identified as a Cistercian monk, but the second is much harder to place. He also looks a bit like a monk—he's wearing a long "monastic mantle," but in addition to that, he's got on chain mail and is carrying a double-edged dagger. So who is this guy? Is he a monk or is he a soldier? Turns out, he's a little of both—because he's one of the Knights Templar, a special order of monks responsible for safeguarding pilgrims on their way to the Holy Lands.

At this point, all of your readerly senses should be tingling. The beginning of the novel is unfolding exactly as you'd expect: Old wounds, which have never really healed, are in danger of being reopened. So you might wonder: How bad will it get before it gets better? Can these new strangers be run out of town? Will the larger conflict between Normans and Saxons finally be resolved?

My main point here is that, after 10 lectures on the art of reading, all of this stuff should seem very familiar. These are just the sorts of questions we've been asking since the start of our course.

The beginning of *Ivanhoe* actually covers about 5 or 6 chapters. In those chapters, the two new strangers make their way to the home of "Cedric the Saxon." (His household, Cedric's household, includes the swineherd and the jester, by the way.)

You can imagine what happens next. One of the strangers (the monk) is friendly and affable. He mostly tries to smooth things over with Cedric, but the other stranger—the Templar—is itching for a fight. He says lots of insulting things about the Saxons and really seems determined to upset and offend his host.

Through these chapters, we're also introduced to some other strangers: First, there's a pilgrim. This man has acted as a guide for the monk and the Templar, helping them to make their way through the woods.

 ©2009 The Teaching Company.

Then there's Isaac, a Jewish traveler, who is seeking refuge from a storm. He is admitted to Cedric's house, but not exactly welcomed there. Indeed, only the mysterious pilgrim or guide shows him any real hospitality.

Here we have a good example of how subplots are introduced and developed. Instead of just one stranger, as in a short story, we have four. In each case, the situation is slightly different.

Take the pilgrim. He's up to something—he won't give his name, and neither will the narrator. So when will his identity be revealed? What about Isaac? Will there ever be a place for him at the table, or will he remain something of an outcast? If there is supposed to be some sort of reconciliation between contending ethnic and social groups, will he and his people be included?

Yet even as these questions proliferate, and even as the subplots pile up, we can see that they are all variations on a very familiar pattern. In each case, it's really just another instance of "stranger comes to town."

I think that's enough to get you started with *Ivanhoe*. So, what about *Jane Eyre*? Do any of our old tricks work with that novel? Of course, they do. We've already discovered, as the result of our prereading, that *Jane Eyre* makes use of the three-part, triple-decker format popularized by Scott. So we have also begun to sense the novel's attachment to a very familiar conception of plot: one that recognizes the importance of beginnings, middles, and endings.

So how does the novel begin? How many strangers do we see this time? Actually, not many—for as it turns out, Brontë is using our other major "master plot": "the hero takes a journey." By the end of the novel, Jane will have moved in and out of five different settings. As we'll see, her journey will be both physical and spiritual.

For now, though, let's just say a few words about some more obvious aspects of the novel. First, unlike *Ivanhoe*, it's written in the first person: The story of Jane Eyre will be told by Jane Eyre. As a result, we feel an intimate connection with this narrator and with the book itself.

As the first chapter begins, we're told a bit about the setting: It's cold and wet, and the nasty weather has forced the characters to stay inside. The weather isn't described in great detail—just enough to give us a little chill of our own. Because we've learned how to connect description to characterization, we can see how quickly Brontë is moving to establish the unpleasantness of Jane's situation.

The household is run by a woman named Mrs. Reed, who has three children about Jane's age. There are no references to Jane's mother or father, which is our first clue that she may be an orphan. (That's always a good guess in a Victorian novel, by the way.)

Before we get to the end of the first page, we learn that Jane has been excluded from the domestic circle. The other children are gathered around their mother, but Mrs. Reed insists that Jane be kept at a distance, explaining that the privileges of intimacy are reserved only for happy children.

So from the start, Jane is blamed for her own isolation. It's her fault that she's alone and unwanted. If she were happier, more contented, she'd deserve a place among the group. But since she's not—she doesn't.

All of this is presented to us on the very first page. It's a terrific, engaging opening. It also serves the purpose of aligning or identifying us with Jane. By the time we've gotten to the end of that page, we're rooting for her—big time.

Here, as we've done so many times before, we might play another round of "what if?" So, what if Jane were offered the chance to join the family circle—and then, quite firmly, refused to do so? What if Mrs. Reed had dropped the bit about "happy children"? What if the other kids were more attractive and likable? (They are, for the record, just dreadful: fat, spoiled, greedy, stupid—they're awful.)

In any of those cases, we might find ourselves withholding sympathy from Jane, wondering if we really wanted to take her side. But because this is a first-person story, and because Jane is placed in the middle of an undeniably awful situation, we don't hesitate for a moment. As I said before, we are rooting for her—big time.

So what about her journey? Where and how does it begin? I suppose you could say that it starts on that very first page, when we see that Jane will never find a secure or comfortable place with the Reeds.

The journey begins in earnest, however, at the start of chapter 5. There, Jane finally gets to leave the Reeds and move away to school. This, however, is hardly a dream come true. The schoolmaster is cold and unfeeling—at one point, he tells Jane that she has a "wicked heart" and "must pray to God to change it."

This is, as I've noted, only the first of several such departures. In chapter 11, Jane leaves school for a position as a governess. Around chapter 25, she leaves that position, despite being "absolutely destitute" and having nowhere else to go. After that—well, that's enough for now, I think.

What can we make of all this? For starters, we can see that here—as in *Ivanhoe*—lessons from earlier lectures have some direct application. This novel is longer and more complicated than almost all of our earlier examples. Yet, beneath the surface, we can find a simple, familiar structure: "the hero takes a journey."

But let's not stop there. Let's push on—and try to come up with a more exact description of this particular journey. What is Jane looking for? What does she want out of life, and why does she have so much trouble finding it?

Such questions first occurred to us in our discussion of characters and characterization—that was back in Lecture Four. At this point, we should be able to see how an emphasis on the character's inner conflicts and personal struggles can produce what's sometimes called a "character-driven novel."

My sense is that Jane wants what most of us want: She wants not to be abused. She wants to be treated with respect. She wants to be accepted for who and what she is. She will keep moving, keep going, until she gets those things. The end of her journey won't come until she finds a place she can call home.

But we shouldn't stop there, either, because that makes it sound as if all of Jane's problems are caused by other people. That makes it seem as if she'll be OK as soon as she moves in with some nicer folks—and that's just not true.

At times, Jane is her own worst enemy. She can be passionate and rebellious, and she sometimes says and does things she later regrets. At times, she would give anything to be rid of those feelings. At times, she really wishes she could be meek and mild, submissive and forgiving, like some of her best friends at school.

So here again, we are reminded of ideas and insights from earlier lectures. For what we see is that Jane not only wants what she can't have—she wants to be what she can never be. Her desires are in conflict. She is torn between what she wants and what she wants to want.

So, without knowing the ending, we can already identify Jane's journey as a quest for self-mastery, self-respect, and self-acceptance. To reach a happy ending, Jane needs something more than a home—and something more than the love of others, too. What she needs, corny as it sounds, is inner peace.

This assessment helps us to see the universality of Jane's story. Most of us do want what Jane wants, and most of us do need what she needs. Maybe that's why, after all these years, the book remains such a great read.

As we look back on this lecture, I hope a few things are clear.

First, I'd like you to see that novels do need to be approached carefully. As you can tell, I'm a big fan of prereading—leafing through the book to get a sense of its organization or structure.

Second, I want you to have confidence in what you've learned so far. For while novels are longer and more complicated than short stories, you already possess most of the tools you'll need to get started. You know how to look for destabilizing events and how to recognize master plots like "stranger" and "hero."

Finally, I hope you realize that your skills can be applied to a wide variety of fictional works. As I noted at the very beginning of this lecture, these two novels could hardly be more different. One is plot-driven; the other is character-driven. One is historical and political; the other is private and personal. Yet, as we've seen, both works can be analyzed, and read, and enjoyed in much the same way.

Not bad for a first effort at novel reading, if I do say so myself. Next time, we'll up the ante and raise the bar, looking at a pair of imposing works from the Age of Modernism.

Thanks as always for joining us. We'll look forward to seeing you next time.

©2009 The Teaching Company.

Lecture Twelve
The Plot Vanishes—Faulkner and Woolf

Scope:

In this lecture, we close out the first part of our course by exploring two highly original, almost experimental works of fiction. These works—*As I Lay Dying*, by William Faulkner, and *The Waves*, by Virginia Woolf—deliberately and dramatically break with the traditions established by authors like Scott and Brontë. At times, in fact, these works may appear to dispense with conventional approaches to characterization and plotting: It is often difficult to tell who is who, to see what is going on, or to separate fact from fantasy. For many readers, the first response to such works is confusion—and unfortunately, frustration, resignation, and defeat. What is the purpose of these literary experiments? And why should we stick with books like these? What do they tell us about how reading works and what reading can do for us?

Outline

I. I decided to close the first half of the course by looking at the sort of book that might strike many of you as almost unreadable.

   A. I am thinking here of novels from the early part of the 20th century: the age of modernism.

   B. Modernist works are innovative and experimental.

   C. If these works are so unconventional, then what are they doing in our course?

   D. We will be discussing *As I Lay Dying*, by William Faulkner, and *The Waves*, by Virginia Woolf.

II. In dealing with both Faulkner and Woolf, I am going to stress the value of prereading. How might you apply this technique to *As I Lay Dying*?

   A. You could start with the title. Who is the "I" in *As I Lay Dying*?

   B. What do we see as we begin to look over the text itself? The book is divided into small pieces; already we can sense that the world of this novel is fragmented.

C. The opening paragraphs in two of three of those first few sections help us to get a handle on narration and style. It looks like first-person narration after all, and this work has multiple narrators.

D. That is a lot to get out of a little prereading, but the first few pages of a novel like *As I Lay Dying* are almost always the most challenging.

III. On to Woolf and what prereading might do for our initial understanding of *The Waves*.

A. The title reminds you of the ocean. The ocean seems to have no beginning and no ending, but the whole point of a story is that it takes us from beginning to middle to end. How does this fit?

B. The text is alternating short sections in italics and longer sections in regular type—a pattern reminiscent of waves.

C. There are no chapter headings like in *As I Lay Dying*, but she does seem to be doing something with those typefaces.

D. What do we see when we take our first look at the nonitalicized sections? Those sections appear to be composed almost entirely of dialogue; there is no description or narration.

E. We can tell that the novel will work largely through contrasts, and we also sense that the natural world of the short, italicized sections will be played off against the human world of longer, nonitalicized ones.

IV. If the author intended to confuse and disorient us, should we not respect those intentions and submit to that confusion—for a little while, at least?

A. If you wanted to wait and do your prereading after taking a first pass through the opening chapters or sections, that would not bother me.

B. But I would not want you to think of prereading as cheating. I think of it as being responsible.

C. In support of that point, we return to *The Waves*—and in particular to the longer, nonitalicized sections of the novel.

V. I conclude with three larger points.

A. Modernist works are difficult. They do not obey the conventions established in earlier periods.

B. Modernist works are not completely unconventional. They establish their own conventions.

C. Modernist works are not really unreadable.

VI. Does the fact that you can read these authors really mean that you should read them?

A. Absolutely. For one thing, they do amazing things with language.

B. In addition, these writers offer amazing insights into human psychology.

Suggested Reading:

Smiley, *13 Ways of Looking at the Novel*, chap. 7.

Whitworth, *Virginia Woolf*, chap. 3.

Questions to Consider:

1. Are you able to enjoy a book that you do not understand completely? Would it bother you to know that there are some passages in Faulkner and Woolf that no one seems to understand completely? If so, why?

2. Why would a writer use multiple narrators? What would happen if you took a work with a single narrator—like *Ivanhoe* or *Jane Eyre*—and rewrote it as a work with multiple narrators? Would the story get more interesting, or would it simply get more confusing?

Lecture Twelve—Transcript
The Plot Vanishes—Faulkner and Woolf

Hello, and welcome to Lecture Twelve in our course on the "art of reading."

Lately, we've been trying to collect our thoughts and apply our new skills to more and more challenging works of fiction. We began with the Sherlock Holmes stories and then moved on to *Ivanhoe* and *Jane Eyre*. That was a pretty logical progression.

So what's next? How can we kick it up a notch and take it to the next level?

As I was I planning the course, I thought about that question for quite a while. I really wanted this lecture to feel like a culmination: I thought it should leave you with a sense of accomplishment and satisfaction.

So I decided to close the first half of the course by looking at the sort of book that might strike many of you as almost unreadable: the sort of book you might put down after only a few pages—or maybe be afraid to pick up in the first place.

I'm thinking here of novels from the early part of the 20th century: the Age of Modernism. This period is usually said to begin around 1913 and run until the end of the 1930s. It includes writers like James Joyce, Marcel Proust, and Gertrude Stein.

Modernist works are innovative and experimental. They break with tradition, approaching familiar tasks in entirely new ways. They're the literary equivalents of Cubist paintings or 12-tone compositions.

So, as I say, these works tend to be fairly intimidating. The first page may sound like gibberish or baby talk. I'm thinking here of *A Portrait of the Artist as a Young Man* by Joyce. Or the narrator may seem to be some sort of lunatic. This time, I'm thinking of *The Sound and the Fury* by William Faulkner.

In these novels and many others like them, we seem to dispense with traditional approaches to characterization and plotting. It's hard to tell who's who—and even harder to see what's going on. In fact, Modernist novels may not seem to have much of a plot at all: Trivial events may be discussed at great length, obscuring big events or relegating them to the margins.

©2009 The Teaching Company.

So, if these works are so unconventional—if the whole concept of plot seems to vanish as we make our way through them—then what are they doing in our course? Are we really ready for them? How do we know that they'll be worth our time and trouble?

Good questions, as usual—but let me assure you that you don't need to worry. You already know enough to make a very good start with these works. Indeed, I'd be prepared to say that if you can handle *Sherlock Holmes* and *Jane Eyre*—and you know that you can—you are ready to take on these new challenges. The ideas and the techniques that you picked up in our first 11 lectures—they really will pay off for you here. Trust me.

OK. I think that's enough of a prologue. At this point, it's time to reveal the titles of the works we'll be discussing. There are two of them: *As I Lay Dying* by Faulkner and *The Waves* by Virginia Woolf.

Both of these novels might be described as late Modernist works: *As I Lay Dying* was published in 1930, after *The Sound and the Fury*—but before *The Bear*, the long story that we discussed in Lecture Six.

The Waves was published in 1931, after more famous and more accessible works like *Mrs. Dalloway* and *To the Lighthouse*.

So these works come about 110 years after *Ivanhoe* and about 80 years after *Jane Eyre*. In other words, there's a pretty big gap between the novels in Lecture Eleven and the novels in Lecture Twelve.

The first thing you might notice, comparing all four of the books, is that the 19th-century novels are much longer than the 20th-century works. By comparison with *Ivanhoe* and *Jane Eyre*, these new works are lean and mean, slender and graceful. *As I Lay Dying* comes in at about 260 pages—*The Waves* at about 290.

That's not uncommon for works of this period. A few Modernist classics (like *Ulysses*) are very, very long. But most (including works by Hemingway, Fitzgerald, Forster, and others) are relatively short. So why is that? Why shouldn't ambitious and experimental books also be sprawling and expansive ones? My sense is that it has something to do with changes in publishing practices and reading habits.

As you'll recall, the 19th century was the heyday of the "triple decker." Through most of that period, novels were published in three-volume sets and read one volume at a time. So, you'd go to the

library, check out volume 1, read it, return it, check out volume 2—
and keep going that way until you were finished.

Under those conditions, your reading experience was almost sure to
be interrupted. What if someone else has checked out volume 2?
What if you decide that, instead of reading volume 3, you'll just
move on to some other novel?

By the time you get to the 1930s, that whole system of publishing,
that whole way of reading—it's long gone. Indeed, to most
sophisticated writers and readers of the Modernist Period, the triple-
decker seems outdated, old-fashioned, and obsolete.

So, as if to announce their departure from Victorian conventions, the
Modernists embraced the values of concentration, intensity, and
rigor—producing much shorter works in the process.

They didn't necessarily expect their readers to finish those works in
one or two sittings—but they may have assumed (or at least hoped)
that reading would cease to involve so much stopping and starting.
For the Modernists, reading should be like watching a play or
listening to a concert: It should require and reward your full,
undivided attention.

If I were you, I would try to respect the wishes of these Modernist
authors. Instead of trying to fit their books into a busy schedule, save
the books for a long weekend—or some time when you can devote
two or three consecutive days to really heavy reading. This time, I'm
afraid, multitasking just isn't going to work for you. To make
headway with Faulkner or Woolf, you'll need to monotask.

While I'm at it, I'd like to offer another piece of advice: Try to read
these books on the "buddy system." They may not be great choices
for everyone in your book club. But if the club includes one or two
fearless readers—people who enjoy a challenge and aren't easily
discouraged—you might think of teaming up with them.

One good approach might be to split up the major characters: You
take a few of them, while your reading partner focuses on a few
others. What should you be looking for? By now, you know the
answer to that: conflicts, reckonings with the past and the self, some
threat to a cherished self-image—all of the things, in other words,
that we started to catalog back in Lecture Four.

    ©2009 The Teaching Company.

I can't say enough about the potential payoff of this activity. In all honesty, I think it could be huge. Modernist fiction tends to be character-driven, so it only makes sense for you to be thinking about characters and characterization.

Up to now, we've been stressing the features or qualities common to both Faulkner and Woolf. In the rest of the lecture, I'd like to treat these works separately. I'll begin by walking you through the experience of getting started with *As I Lay Dying*. Then, I'll do the same thing with *The Waves*.

I figure that's the best way of helping you to get over those initial feelings of frustration and bewilderment—and the best way of convincing you that, although these books may be daunting, you really should be confident of your ability to enjoy and appreciate them.

In dealing with both Faulkner and Woolf, I'm going to stress the value of "prereading." As you'll recall, prereading is a technique that lets you take a bird's eye view of the entire work before plunging into the first chapter.

So, how might you apply this technique to *As I Lay Dying*? You could start with the title. We talked about titles a little bit in Lecture Seven, right?

OK, then, who is the "I" in *As I Lay Dying*? Will this be a first-person narrative? Will one of the characters actually be preparing for death? If so, will that character spend most of the novel looking back over his or her life?

At this point, we can't be sure of the answers to any of these questions. But for now, that's OK—because all we're really trying to do here is get our minds warmed up. We'd like to generate some possibilities, give ourselves something to look out for. Already, even at this early stage, we've got it: We need to look for a character who is dying.

We might also begin to wonder how that death will affect the other characters. Will it come as a surprise or a shock? Will it come as a relief? Will those other characters make peace with each other, or will some of their issues remain unresolved?

Not bad for the title page. What do we see as we begin to look over the text itself? Here, I might remind you, we're not reading so much as eyeballing the text—trying to get a sense of what it includes and how it's organized.

What we see is that *As I Lay Dying* is divided into small pieces. The first one is not even two pages long; the next one runs for about three pages, total; the one after that for another three pages.

So, what are we to make of that? Already we can sense that the world of this novel is fragmented, maybe even shattered. It may be the kind of world in which people see or approach things in fundamentally different ways—the kind in which worldviews can be said to be incommensurate with each other.

If this world can be put back together—and that's a big if—it may take a long time and may require a lot of effort. Even then, there's probably no guarantee of success.

That's a good start—a very good start, as a matter of fact. At this point, you might notice that you're using the same terms and the same techniques that you've been using all along. These works are different, but our approach to them doesn't really have to be.

There is one more thing to say about those pieces or fragments in *As I Lay Dying*, however. Each one has some kind of heading. The headings are in bold type and capital letters, and that has the effect of setting them off from the rest of the text.

The first heading is "Darl." That's "D-A-R-L": "Darl." The second is "Cora." Then it's "Darl" again; then "Jewel"; then "Darl" again.

Since Cora is a person's name, and Jewel can be a name, we might assume that Darl is also a name. It's still too early to tell if Darl is male or female, however. If Darl is a name, there's no way of knowing why it appears at the beginning of so many of those early sections. Maybe Darl is the person who's dying—or someone closely related to that person.

At this point, we might want to stop eyeballing and do a little bit of actual reading. We're still not reading too deeply—maybe just looking at the opening paragraphs in two or three of those first few sections.

What will this tell us? For starters, it will help us to get a handle on narration. In looking at the title, we thought we might be dealing

©2009 The Teaching Company.

with a first-person narrator. So, if we see a lot of "I-statements" in those opening paragraphs, we'll know that we were right.

In addition, a look at those opening paragraphs will help us to get a feel for Faulkner's style. Given what we've learned about his penchant for "maximalism," we might expect to see lots of very long sentences. But who knows? Maybe that's not the only trick he has up his sleeve. Maybe he's perfectly capable of writing in some other way.

Fair enough. If we look at the openings of several sections, we'll see what kind of narrator—and what kind of style—he's using this time. (Narration and style—doesn't that sound familiar?)

OK, so what do we see in these openings? The opening to the first section begins this way: "Jewel and I come up from the field."

The opening to the second section goes like this: "So I saved out the eggs and baked yesterday."

So, it looks like we are dealing with first-person narration after all. Indeed, the openings to the third, and fourth, and fifth sections also include lots of I-statements.

It's not clear that all of those statements are coming from the same person, however. By now, in fact, it's pretty obvious that this work has multiple narrators: The first section is narrated by Darl, the second by Cora, the third by Darl again, and so on. We touched on this possibility in Lecture Three, so it shouldn't come as a complete surprise.

What about style? Each of the narrators seems to have a style of his or her own. Darl is generally direct and straightforward—though there are times when he lets himself go. Cora is a chatterbox, and Jewel is violent and profane. You'll see those differences immediately if you let yourself read little bits of each section out loud.

Since none of these narrators qualifies as a maximalist—there are no sprawling two- or three-page sentences here—it must be that Faulkner is up to something else. Maybe, in this work, he's trying to show that he's a master of many styles—able to move in and out of many different voices.

In any case, we can sense that if this world is fragmented, if it is splintered into small bits and pieces—that's probably because its people can't agree on what's important or even on what sort of language to use in describing it.

I know—that's a lot to get out of a little bit of prereading. But as I've been saying from the start, I think you can do it, too. I know that it'll help. The first few pages of a novel like *As I Lay Dying* are almost always the most challenging—and if you can go into them with a few solid hunches about what to expect, you will be much more likely to hang in there to the end.

That's enough on Faulkner—at least for now. So let's move on to Woolf and see what prereading might do for our initial understanding of *The Waves*.

Why don't we start with the title? That's where we started with Faulkner, right? This title reminds you of the ocean. The waves come in and go out again. They've been doing that forever, and they'll go on doing it long after you and I are gone.

So, perhaps this title will diminish the importance of human concerns and human time—and so, perhaps, will the entire work. The waves are eternal—we are not.

When you think about it in that way, you may begin to wonder what Woolf is up to here. She can't be writing a novel about the ocean, can she? If she is, what kind of novel would that be? What kinds of characters would appear in it? What kinds of stories could it tell?

Look at it this way: The thing about the ocean is that it seems to have no beginning and no ending. The whole point of a story, as we saw in Lecture Eight, is that it takes us from beginning, to middle, to end. So how can these two things—the ocean and storytelling—possibly be fit together? Very interesting questions, questions that confound—maybe even challenge—our sense of what a story can be.

What's next, then? Eyeballing the text—looking it over to get a sense of how it's set up, structured, and organized.

If you open *The Waves*, the very first thing you'll see is a very short section in italics: a page and a half—that' s it. Then there's a longer section in regular type—about 20 pages this time. After that, another one of those short, italicized sections—and then another, much longer, section in regular type.

So, does it go on like that until we get to the end? You got it! Yes, indeed—it does. So this time, we have a kind of alternating pattern: short, long, short, long. Really, it's two patterns because in addition

©2009 The Teaching Company.

to varying the length of the sections, Woolf also varies their layout or look: italics, no italics, italics, no italics.

What does all that make you think of? It makes me think of the title, *The Waves*—something coming in, and going out, and coming in again. So perhaps we were wrong to be skeptical. Perhaps Woolf will find a way of blending the movement of the ocean with the movement of her book.

When we looked at *As I Lay Dying*, we wondered about those chapter headings. You remember "Darl," "Cora," "Darl." Does Woolf give us anything like that? No—as a matter of fact, she doesn't.

But as we've already begun to notice, she does seem to be doing something with those typefaces. So, what if we skip from one italicized section to the next? Just how do those sections begin? What, if anything, do they have in common?

Here's the first line of the first one: "The sun had not yet risen." Here's the first line of the second one: "The sun rose higher." Already you can begin to predict the sort of thing you'll see in the later ones: "The sun had risen to its full height." "The sun was sinking"—and so on.

Here, then, is another eternal cycle: sunrise and sunset—but somehow, this one seems to have a more definite beginning and ending. It's a little easier for us human beings to understand or comprehend. The sun rises in the morning—or seems to—and goes down again at night. In reality, of course, the sun isn't going anywhere, which may mean that Woolf is hinting at the human tendency to impose patterns on otherwise formless, natural processes.

So, is that all there is to those italicized sections? No, in fact, it's not. If you read into them a bit further, you'll see that—in addition to the sun—they mention all kinds of other things: birds, rocks, sand, wheat fields—and, of course, the waves.

You'll also notice that these sections are rendered in a poetic, lyrical style. Let me give you a quick taste of that. I want you to hear it for yourself.

This is from the second italicized section, the one that begins with "The sun rose higher":

"Blue waves, green waves swept a quick fan over the beach, circling the spike of sea-holly and leaving shallow pools of light here and there on the sand. A faint black rim was left behind them." Only two sentences here—and yet they say so much.

In the first sentence, the quickness of the waves is suggested by the quickness of the language. Instead of "blue waves and green waves" or "blue and green waves," we get "blue waves, green waves"—just a comma between the phrases.

In the second sentence, that quickness is gone. What's left behind? Something a little duller, a little dimmer—expressed almost entirely in monosyllables: "A faint black rim was left behind them."

So much for the italicized sections. Before moving on to the others— that is, to the sections in regular type—I might note that you could take what we've been doing with Woolf and try it out on Faulkner. If you read several "Darl" sections back to back, you'll certainly gain some valuable insights into his character.

OK, then. What about the other half of *The Waves*? What do we see when we take our first look at the non-italicized sections?

Those sections appear to be composed almost entirely of dialogue. There's no description of any kind—no blue waves, no green waves, nothing—and, aside from the speech tags, no narration, either.

The tags, it might be noted, are as flat and unremarkable as they can be. What's more, they're all exactly alike: Every single time it's always "said Neville" or "said Jinny." It's never "remarked Jinny" or "observed Jinny."

So, already our prereading is starting to bear fruit. We can tell that *The Waves* will work largely through contrasts, and we can also sense that the natural world of the short, italicized sections will be played off against the human world of the longer, non-italicized ones.

At this point, you might have some questions for me: Isn't this cheating? Doesn't it make it all a little too easy? After all, if these great authors intended to confuse and disorient us, shouldn't we respect their intentions and submit to that confusion—for a little while, at least?

Look, I think those are reasonable questions, and if you want to wait and do your prereading after taking a first pass through the opening chapters or sections, that's not going to bother me.

©2009 The Teaching Company.

But I wouldn't want you to think of this as cheating. I think of it as being responsible.

Instead of diving in and floundering around, you're taking time to look and see what the author has done. You're gathering some impressions of the larger structure, sizing up the work as a whole, before beginning to scrutinize any of the parts.

It seems to me, in fact, that a technique like prereading gives you a much better chance of recognizing and appreciating the author's achievements. Besides, even if you do preread, you'll have ample opportunities for confusion later on. You can trust me on that one.

In support of that point, I'll take us back to *The Waves*—and in particular to the longer, non-italicized sections of the novel—because if confusion is what you want, you're likely to get plenty of it there.

I already told you that these sections are composed almost entirely of dialogue. What I didn't tell you was that the dialogue in this novel is bizarre. It doesn't sound like anything you would ever say out loud— unless you were in the habit of verbalizing your sense impressions.

In the first of these bizarre speeches, a character named Bernard says: "I see a ring ... hanging above me. It quivers and hangs in a loop of light."

See what I mean? That's not even a thought—much less a bit of dialogue.

After Bernard is finished, a character named Susan chimes in: "I see a slab of pale yellow," she says, "spreading away until it meets a purple stripe."

What's next? Four more characters tell what they see or hear. Some characters are—in order—Neville, Jinny, and Louis.

Just when we're starting to get the hang of this, the cycle starts all over again. It repeats almost five times in the space of three pages. Through it all, we never find out how old these people are—nor do we find out what they look like, or what they're wearing, or even where they're standing. Are they supposed to be on the beach, watching the sunrise? It doesn't really seem like it, but it's hard to tell.

At the beginning of this lecture, I said that Modernist writers often broke with Victorian conventions. This is the sort of thing I had in mind.

Nineteenth-century writers like Scott and Brontë, they made sure that their readers had a clear image of each new character. The characters would be described from head to toe. They would also be placed in a social network or hierarchy: This is the swineherd; this is the jester; this is the monk and the Templar.

Almost all of that vanishes when we get to writers like Faulkner and Woolf. In a novel from the Age of Modernism, it can take a long, long time to figure out who the characters are—and even longer to nail down their relationships to each other.

For example, in the first section of *As I Lay Dying*, Darl says that he came up from the field with a person named Jewel. (We quoted that passage earlier, right?) OK—but who is Jewel? Maybe more importantly, who is he to Darl? Are they friends? Relatives? Strangers?

As it turns out, they're brothers—but it takes a long, long while for that fact to become clear. In reality, they're actually half-brothers. That's another story, though, and one we don't need to worry about right now.

In fact, I don't think we need to worry about much of anything at this point. We've already done more than enough to get you started on these works—and so, instead of providing further details, I'd like to conclude with two or three larger points.

Point number one: Modernist works are difficult—no two ways about it. They don't obey the conventions established in earlier periods.

Point number two: Modernist works are not completely unconventional. It's probably more accurate to say that they establish their own conventions—inventing new ways of introducing characters or developing a plot.

If we had more time, you'd see that these works also observe many of the old conventions as well. They still employ description. They still have beginnings, middles, and endings. They still follow age-old patterns. *As I Lay Dying* is a great example of "hero takes a journey."

Point number three: Modernist works are not really unreadable. In fact, as I said earlier, you already know how to handle them. You can preread. You can ask questions and make hypotheses. You can keep a list of the characters—and maybe in the case of *As I Lay Dying*— work up some kind of family tree for them.

 ©2009 The Teaching Company.

So it's true: If you can handle *Sherlock Holmes* and *Jane Eyre*, you really are ready for Faulkner and Woolf—even when their characters start to say things like "I see a slab of pale yellow."

One last question may remain, however: Does the fact that you can read these authors really mean that you *should* read them? Can I guarantee that Faulkner and Woolf will be worth the effort? Absolutely. For one thing, these writers do amazing things with language. You've already gotten a taste of Woolf's intensely lyrical style, so you should be ready to agree with me on that point.

In case you're wavering, let me just give you another brief example.

This comes from near the end of the novel. Here, Woolf's narrator makes a simple but powerful analogy between the onset of darkness and the movement of the ocean:

> As if there were waves of darkness in the air, darkness moved on, covering houses, hills, trees, as waves of water wash round the sides of some sunken ship. Darkness washed down streets eddying round single figures, engulfing them; blotting out couples clasped under the showery darkness of elm trees in full summer foliage.

Now wouldn't it be a shame to miss out on something like that?

In addition, these writers offer amazing insights into human psychology. They show us how we think—how in a moment our minds can go from memory, to rationalization, to fantasy.

If you don't mind, just one last example from *The Waves*. This also comes from the end. Here, one of the characters (Bernard) reflects on the passage of time:

> Should this be the end of the story? a kind of sigh? a last ripple of the wave? A trickle of water to some gutter where, burbling, it dies away? Let me touch the table—so—and thus recover my sense of the moment. A sideboard covered with cruets; a basket full of rolls; a plate of bananas—these are comfortable sights. But if there are no stories, what end can there be, or what beginning? Life is not susceptible perhaps to the treatment we give it when we try to tell it.

Just look at that. Woolf shows us how this man works to reassure himself—how he feels for the table, as if to put himself back in touch with reality. She also has him reflect on the nature of storytelling. Just look at how many concepts from our earlier lectures are packed into that passage: endings; beginnings; the possibility that stories are, by definition, unrealistic.

So, yes—I guarantee it. From time to time, you may feel uncertain or even frustrated. But in the end, you won't be sorry that you took on these challenges.

I certainly do hope that this lecture has seemed like something of a culmination for you, that it's helped you to see the value of what we've been doing together. Over and over again, concepts and techniques from earlier lectures have come together to enrich our experience of reading.

What's in store for us in the second part of the course? What aspects of fiction, and what kinds of reading, await us in Lectures Thirteen to Twenty-Four?

Please don't ask me that. You know how I hate to spoil the ending.

Thanks as always for joining us. It has been a great pleasure. We'll look forward to seeing you soon.

©2009 The Teaching Company.

Timeline

1771 ....Sir Walter Scott born in
                       Edinburgh, Scotland.

1775 ....Jane Austen born in
                       Hampshire, England.

1812 ....Charles Dickens born in
                       Hampshire, England.

1816 ....Charlotte Brontë born in
                       Yorkshire, England.

1818 ....*Persuasion*, Jane Austen.

1819 ....*Ivanhoe*, Sir Walter Scott.

1828 ....Leo Tolstoy born in Tula Province,
                       Russian empire.

1835 ....Samuel Clemens (Mark Twain) born
                       in Missouri.

1840 .... Thomas Hardy born in
                       Dorset, England.

1843 .... Henry James born in
                       New York City.

1843 ....*A Christmas Carol*,
                       Charles Dickens.

1847 ....*Jane Eyre*, Charlotte Brontë.

1852–1853...................................*Bleak House*, Charles Dickens.

1857 ....Joseph Conrad born in
                       Berdichev, Ukraine.

1859 ....Sir Arthur Conan Doyle born in
                       Edinburgh, Scotland.

1860–1861...................................*Great Expectations*,
                       Charles Dickens.

1862 ....Edith Wharton born in
                       New York City.

1865–1869	*War and Peace*, Leo Tolstoy.
1866	H. G. Wells born in Kent, England.
1873	Willa Cather born in Virginia.
1881	P. G. Wodehouse born in Surrey, England.
1882	Virginia Woolf born in London, England.
1885	*The Adventures of Huckleberry Finn*, Mark Twain.
1886	*The Mayor of Casterbridge*, Thomas Hardy.
1887	*A Study in Scarlet*, Sir Arthur Conan Doyle.
1890	*The Sign of Four*, Sir Arthur Conan Doyle.
1892	*The Adventures of Sherlock Holmes*, Sir Arthur Conan Doyle.
1894	*The Memoirs of Sherlock Holmes*, Sir Arthur Conan Doyle.
1896	F. Scott Fitzgerald born in Minnesota.
1897	William Faulkner born in Mississippi.
1898	*The Turn of the Screw*, Henry James.
1898	*The War of the Worlds*, H. G. Wells.
1899	*Heart of Darkness*, Joseph Conrad.
1903	Evelyn Waugh born in London, England.
1918	*My Ántonia*, Willa Cather.
1920	*The Age of Innocence*, Edith Wharton.

©2009 The Teaching Company.

Glossary

ambiguity: Uncertainty of meaning. An ambiguous line or passage is one that can be interpreted in at least two ways.

beginning, middle, and end: Essential elements of any narrative, according to Aristotle's *Poetics*. Beginnings introduce us to important characters and suggest the presence of buried conflicts. Middles feature the complications of those conflicts. And endings present their resolutions.

destabilizing event: The event that kicks off a narrative, usually by exposing a problem and knocking the characters off balance.

formalist approach: Focuses on the formal elements of a work, including its plot, structure, and style. Often distinguished from biographical and historicist approaches.

free indirect discourse (f.i.d.): A term used to describe passages in which a third-person narrator appears to borrow words or phrases from the characters. Often used to give the reader a sense of how a character is reacting to an unfolding scene.

genre: Literary critical term for "kind" or "type" or "category." Types, or genres, of prose fiction include detective stories, westerns, legal thrillers, and family sagas.

implied author: Term coined by theorist Wayne C. Booth to describe the authorial figure created or constructed in a work of literature. Our most important relationship is to this figure, Booth argues, and not to the actual, flesh-and-blood writer.

irony: Like ambiguity, a device that allows for the possibility of multiple shades of meaning. Theorists usually distinguish between verbal irony (a property of words) and dramatic irony (a property of the events or scenes in a narrative). Verbal irony results from a discrepancy between the usual meaning of a word and the meaning intended by some particular speaker. Dramatic irony results from another sort of discrepancy. In this case, the tension is between the characters' limited understanding of a situation and the reader's more accurate view.

master plot: A recurring story or narrative, also known as a master narrative or cultural myth. Classic examples might include "hero takes a journey" and "stranger comes to town."

 ©2009 The Teaching Company.

modernism: An early 20th-century movement in the arts marked by intensive, sometimes radical, formal experimentation. Modernist fiction includes works by James Joyce, Virginia Woolf, and William Faulkner.

narrator: The storyteller. Most narrators are first person (as in *Jane Eyre* or *Huck Finn* or *The Catcher in the Rye*) or "third person" (as in *Ivanhoe* or "Runaway" or *The Age of Innocence*). Other possibilities exist, however, including first-person plural and second-person narration.

prereading: A tool for gathering impressions of a book's larger shape, design, or structure. Look at the following: Is it divided into smaller parts? If so, how many are there? How long are they? Are the parts numbered or titled? What does their arrangement or layout imply about the work as a whole?

realism: Generally defined as fidelity to real life, realism is one of the trickiest terms in the literary lexicon. C. S. Lewis distinguished "realism of presentation" (expressed through physical description) from "realism of content" (expressed largely through plotting). Other sorts of realism might include psychological realism and moral realism.

round characters: Characters possessing emotional depth or psychological complexity. For E. M. Forster, who invented this phrase, there was a simple test for roundness: Is the character capable of "surprising in a convincing way"?

scene and summary: Basic building blocks of fictional narrative. Scenes are dominated by dialogue, while summaries are dominated by narration. Summaries might include physical descriptions, background information, and stage directions.

story and plot: Terms devised (or perhaps refined) by the Russian formalists of the early 20th century. If you list the events of a narrative in the order of their original occurrence, you get the "story." If you list those same events in the order of their presentation to the reader, you get the "plot." In many narratives (*As I Lay Dying* or "Runaway" or the Sherlock Holmes stories) the reader's most immediate task is to rearrange the events of the plot into something like a coherent story.

subtext: Emotions lying behind the words and actions in a scene. The subtext is what drives the characters, whether they know it consciously or not.

Biographical Notes

Aristotle (384–322 B.C.E.): One of the foundational figures in Western philosophy. His works address a wide variety of subjects, including ethics, logic, poetics, political theory, and natural science. Born in Stagira, Greece, he was the son of a medical doctor named Nichomacus. Nichomacus died when Aristotle was about 10 years old, leaving him in the care of Proxenus of Atarneus, who continued the boy's education. At age 17, he entered Plato's Academy in Athens. After completing his studies, Aristotle became a teacher at the Academy, holding this post for about 20 years. He left around the time of Plato's death in 347 B.C.E. and traveled to the island of Assos, where he conducted biological research. He returned to Athens, founded a school, and devoted himself to teaching and writing until his retirement in 323 B.C.E. He died of a digestive illness the following year. Among his most important works are *Nicomachean Ethics*, *Politics*, and *Metaphysics*. Especially important for students of literature is the *Poetics* (c. 335 B.C.E.), in which he unfolds his influential theory of catharsis.

Austen, Jane (1775–1817): The most beloved of all novelists. Austen is admired by general readers as well as her fellow artists, and her work has been the subject of countless film and television adaptations. Austen was born in Hampshire, England, the sixth of seven children. Her father was a clergyman. She grew up in a family of devoted novel readers and showed an early talent for satire and parody. Austen began her first serious literary projects while in her 20s, producing early versions of what would later become *Sense and Sensibility* (1811), *Pride and Prejudice* (1813), and *Northanger Abbey* (1818). Other major works include *Mansfield Park* (1814) and *Emma* (1815). *Persuasion* (1818) reflects her great admiration for the Navy—in which two of her brothers served. It was the last novel she finished before her death. Given her interest in courtship, it is worth noting that Austen never married. She did accept one proposal, from a younger man with a considerable fortune. But, for reasons that will probably always remain unclear, she withdrew her acceptance the next day.

©2009 The Teaching Company.

Borges, Jorge Luis (1899–1986): Argentine short story writer, poet, and essayist. Borges grew up in Buenos Aires and moved to Geneva, Switzerland, at the beginning of World War I. He learned English before Spanish and acquired French and German while in Geneva. In 1921, he returned to Buenos Aires and published his first book of poetry. He began writing fiction in the 1930s, producing most of his best work after the death of his father in 1938. Some of his most important stories appeared in *Fictions* (1944), which included "Pierre Menard, Author of the *Quixote*," "The Circular Ruins," and "The Library of Babel." Borges worked at the Buenos Aires library until he was dismissed for political reasons when Juan Perón came to power. After Perón was ousted, Borges was appointed director of the national library and given a professorship at the University of Buenos Aires. By the mid-1950s, a congenital affliction left Borges completely blind. His late works, such as *Dreamtigers* (1960) and *The Book of Sand* (1975), retained a sense of the surreal while effacing the borders between genres.

Brontë, Charlotte (1816–1855): Novelist and poet famous for *Jane Eyre* (1847) and other novels featuring strong heroines at odds with social circumstances. Patrick Brontë, Charlotte's father, was an evangelical Anglican minister who encouraged his children to study natural history and explore the moors surrounding the village. Brontë's mother died when she was five years old. In her adult life, Brontë earned money by teaching in order to help her brother and sisters. In 1846, she published a book of poems along with her sisters Emily and Anne under the pseudonym Currer Bell. She continued to use this pseudonym for her first two novels. In the early 1850s, after the deaths of her three remaining siblings, Brontë traveled to London three times, where she met important literary figures such as William Makepeace Thackeray, Elizabeth Gaskell, and Harriet Martineau. She rejected three proposals before marrying in 1854. She died the following year, most likely due to complications resulting from pregnancy.

Calvino, Italo (1923–1985): Italian short story writer and novelist known for his formally inventive stories and his use of fable and folktale. Calvino was born in Cuba and grew up in San Remo, Italy, on the Italian Riviera. In 1943, Calvino joined the Italian Resistance and fought against the Germans in the Ligurian Mountains. After the war, he studied literature at the University of Turin. In the 1950s, he began writing fantastical and allegorical stories. He gained fame for three novels published in this period: *The Cloven Viscount* (1952),

The Baron in the Trees (1957), and *The Nonexistent Knight* (1959). He also traveled Italy collecting folktales, which he published as *Italian Folktales* (1956). In the late 1960s, Calvino became interested in semiotics and moved to Paris, where he associated with an avant-garde literary group known as Oulipo. In his later works, Calvino employed elaborate constraints to construct novels that address the issues of chance, change, and the act of reading. For example, *If on a winter's night a traveler* (1979) recounts the frustration of you, the reader, attempting to read Italo Calvino's latest book. He died of a cerebral hemorrhage in 1985.

Cather, Willa (1873–1947): American novelist whose work centers on the experiences of settlers in the American West. She was born in Virginia but moved to Nebraska at age nine, where she first met the immigrant settler groups that would factor heavily in her fictions. She attended the University of Nebraska, where she excelled at journalism and story writing. Upon graduating, she supported herself with editorial jobs at various magazines. After writing about cosmopolitan life in her unspectacular debut novel, *Alexander's Bridge* (1912), Cather turned to the pioneer landscape of her childhood for inspiration. Her second novel, *O Pioneers!* (1913), examines the strength of women on the frontier. She returned to this theme in her greatest work, *My Ántonia* (1918), which focuses on the story of a Bohemian immigrant girl who meets with hardships on the Nebraska prairies. Her novel *One of Ours* (1922) won the Pulitzer Prize. Cather began a romantic relationship with the editor Edith Lewis in the early 1900s. The two lived together from 1912 until Cather's death in 1947.

Chekhov, Anton Pavlovich (1860–1904): One of the greatest modern playwrights and short story writers. As a child, Chekhov endured frequent beatings and worked long hours for his father, a grocer who struggled and failed to make a living. After his father went bankrupt, the teenage Chekhov began publishing comic sketches and journalistic pieces in order to support his family while he studied to become a doctor. His stories gradually became more serious over the course of the 1880s, culminating in "Steppe" (1888) and "A Dreary Story" (1889). His most famous story is "The Lady with the Dog" (1899). Chekhov was also a brilliant playwright, and in the period from 1896 to 1903, he produced four dramatic masterpieces: *The Seagull* (1896), *Uncle Vanya* (1899), *Three Sisters* (1901), and *The Cherry Orchard* (1903). He continued to practice medicine throughout his life, claiming, "Medicine is my lawful wife, and literature is my mistress." He died of tuberculosis in 1904. Chekhov's thematic concerns are remarkably various, but his works are unified by formal inventiveness and an unsentimental concern for the mundane aspects of characters' lives.

Coetzee, J. M. (John Maxwell; b. 1940): South African novelist and essayist whose writing frequently addresses issues of colonialism. Coetzee grew up in Cape Town and attended the University of Cape Town, where he studied English and mathematics. He then went on to earn a doctorate from the University of Texas at Austin. He started writing fiction in 1969, publishing his first novel, *Dusklands*, in 1974. His second novel won South Africa's highest literary prize, the CNA, but it was his third novel, *Waiting for the Barbarians* (1980), that established his reputation internationally. Coetzee was the first writer to win two Booker Prizes, first for *The Life and Times of Michael K* (1983) and again for *Disgrace* (1999). *Disgrace* follows a South African university professor as he moves to his daughter's farm after being publicly shamed in a sex scandal. In addition to writing fiction, Coetzee has had a distinguished career as an academic, holding professorships at SUNY Buffalo, the University of Cape Town, Johns Hopkins, Harvard, Stanford, and the University of Chicago. He was awarded the Nobel Prize in Literature in 2003. He currently resides in Adelaide, Australia.

Conan Doyle, Arthur (1859–1930): Novelist and short story writer best known for his Sherlock Holmes detective stories. Conan Doyle was born in Edinburgh and studied medicine at the University of Edinburgh, where he began writing stories. He worked as a physician in Southsea, England, and wrote while waiting for patients, eventually producing his first novel, *A Study in Scarlet* (1887), in which the character of Sherlock Holmes first appeared. The character became enormously popular as Conan Doyle began to write serialized stories featuring Holmes. Hoping to turn to other concerns, Conan Doyle killed Holmes in a story of 1893, but he later resurrected the character due to public outcry. Conan Doyle's writings were remarkably diverse, including propaganda defending the imperial venture in the Boer War, for which he was knighted in 1902; a six-volume *History of the British Campaign in France and Flanders* (1920); a two-volume *History of Spiritualism* (1926); historical novels; science fiction stories; poems; and plays. He died of a heart attack on July 7, 1930. A curious episode from his life, in which he had a chance to play detective, is the basis for Julian Barnes's novel *Arthur and George* (2005).

Conrad, Joseph (1857–1924): A crucial figure in the transition into modernism, valued for his experiments with narrative form and his reflections on the nature of storytelling. Though his parents were both Polish, he was born in Ukraine. He effectively lost his parents at age 5, when they were exiled to a village in northern Russia. Conrad went to sea at 16, visiting the West Indies and Venezuela while serving in the French merchant marine. He later sought work on British ships and became an English subject in 1886. The most important journey of his career came in 1890, when he sailed to the coast of Africa and steamed up the Congo River. This journey would become the basis for his most famous and influential work, *Heart of Darkness* (1899), which would later serve as the inspiration for the film *Apocalypse Now* (1979). Closely associated with other major figures, including Henry James and Ford Madox Ford, Conrad would publish several other important works of fiction, including *Almayer's Folly* (1895); *Lord Jim* (1900); *Nostromo* (1904); *The Secret Agent* (1907), now celebrated as one of the first novels to take up the issue of urban terrorism; and *Under Western Eyes* (1911).

Dickens, Charles (1812–1870): Prolific novelist often considered the greatest writer of the Victorian era. He was born into a middle-class family in Hampshire, England, and moved to Chatham in his infancy. Dickens's father disastrously mismanaged the family's finances. As a result, he was jailed for debt in 1824, and the 12-year-old Charles was taken out of school to work in a factory. As a young adult, Dickens worked as a journalist for various publications. His first stories appeared in magazines in 1832. In 1837, he serialized his first novel, *The Pickwick Papers*, which vaulted him into celebrity and made him the most popular writer of his day. His most famous piece of fiction, *A Christmas Carol*, appeared in 1843. Later novels like *David Copperfield* (1849–1850), *Bleak House* (1852–1853), *Little Dorrit* (1855–1857), and *Great Expectations* (1860–1861) augmented his fame and marked major innovations in English literature. Dickens was renowned for his charismatic public readings, which drew massive audiences. His works are characterized by a concern for industrial laborers and the suffering of children, comic elements and caricatures, and mastery of dialogue in many dialects.

Faulkner, William (1897–1962): Nobel Prize–winning American novelist and short story writer. Faulkner grew up in Oxford, Mississippi, where he learned to ride horses and hunt. He left high school before graduating and joined the British Royal Air Force during World War I after failing to meet U.S. military requirements, but the war ended before he finished training. He returned to Oxford, where he would live for the rest of his life. In 1924, he published a book of pastoral poetry, though he quickly shifted his focus to fiction. His first major breakthrough came in 1929 with *The Sound and the Fury*, which collects four separate stream-of-consciousness monologues. Subsequent novels, such as *As I Lay Dying* (1930) and *Absalom, Absalom!* (1936), built on this development, employing multiple narrators and eschewing narrative closure. In the 1930s and 1940s, Faulkner occasionally supplemented his income by writing screenplays for Hollywood films. His widely anthologized work, *The Bear*, can be found in *Go Down, Moses* (1940). After winning the Nobel Prize in 1950, he wrote less and began to drink more heavily. He died of a heart attack at age 64.

Fitzgerald, F. Scott (1896–1940): American novelist and short story writer of the Jazz Age. Fitzgerald grew up in St. Paul, Minnesota and attended Princeton University. At Princeton, he became an active part of the theatrical and literary life of the university. He performed poorly, however, and flunked out in 1917. After a brief return to Princeton, he joined the army and was stationed in Alabama, where he met Zelda Sayre and began writing his first novel. Fitzgerald fell in love with Zelda, and the two were engaged when he set off to find success in New York. Shortly thereafter, she broke off the engagement, prompting Fitzgerald to return to St. Paul to finish his novel. Published in 1920, *This Side of Paradise* brought him fame and prosperity. He and Zelda married later that year and had a daughter soon after. In 1924, the family moved to the French Riviera, where Fitzgerald wrote his greatest novel, *The Great Gatsby* (1925). Over the next several years, Fitzgerald sank into alcoholism, and Zelda had two mental breakdowns, from which she never fully recovered. In 1937, with his wife in a sanatorium, Fitzgerald moved to Hollywood to become a scriptwriter, remaining there until his death of a heart attack at age 44.

Hardy, Thomas (1840–1928): English novelist and poet known for his darkly pessimistic writing. Hardy grew up in Dorset, England, and spent much of his childhood exploring the surrounding countryside. He dreamed of attending Cambridge and entering the clergy, but instead his parents apprenticed him to an ecclesiastical architect. In the mid-1860s, he turned his attention to literature. Finding his first poems poorly received, Hardy began writing novels. He abandoned architecture in 1872 and published his first major novel, *Far from the Madding Crowd*, in 1874. Of the five novels he published in the following decade, only one, *The Return of the Native* (1878), achieved distinction. His next success came with *The Mayor of Casterbridge* (1886), which addresses class issues and the conflict between urban modernization and rural traditionalism. After the success of *Tess of the d'Urbervilles* (1891) and *Jude the Obscure* (1895), Hardy returned to his first love, poetry. He wrote in a wide variety of forms and meters, including ballads, lyrics, dramatic monologues, and even epic.

Hawthorne, Nathaniel (1804–1864): American novelist and short story writer best known for *The Scarlet Letter* (1850) and *House of the Seven Gables* (1851). Hawthorne was born into a prominent Puritan family in Salem, Massachusetts. His father died when he was four years old. Much of his young life was spent reading and writing fiction. After graduating from Bowdoin College, Hawthorne gained a measure of fame through his short stories but was unable to achieve financial independence through his writing alone. He took a job at the Boston Custom House, eventually saving enough money to marry Sophie Peabody and rent a house in Concord, where he met Ralph Waldo Emerson and Henry David Thoreau. When his stories continued to sell poorly, he returned to Salem, where he wrote *The Scarlet Letter*. From there, he moved to Lenox, where he befriended Herman Melville and wrote *House of the Seven Gables*. His later writing is undistinguished and shows signs of psychological troubles. In his final two years, he suffered frequent nosebleeds and began writing the number 64 obsessively. He died in his sleep in 1864.

Hemingway, Ernest (1899–1961): Novelist and story writer known for his spare, minimalist style. Born in a suburb of Chicago, Hemingway spent his childhood summers hunting and fishing at a family home in northern Michigan. After graduating from high school in 1917, Hemingway worked as a reporter before leaving to join the war effort. Rejected from the army due to his poor vision, he

 ©2009 The Teaching Company.

became a volunteer ambulance driver for the Red Cross. He was injured in 1918 while delivering supplies to troops. While recovering at a hospital in Milan, he fell in love with a nurse who rejected his marriage proposal. In 1921, Hemingway moved to Paris, where he received advice and encouragement from Gertrude Stein and Ezra Pound. His first literary success came in 1925, with the publication of *In Our Time*, a collection of stories including "Big Two-Hearted River." In the following year, he published his first major novel, *The Sun Also Rises*, which tells the story of disaffected expatriates in postwar France and Spain. Hemingway actively supported the Republican cause in the Spanish Civil War and flew missions for the Royal Air Force in World War II. The themes in his books mirror his passions in life: bull-fighting in *Death in the Afternoon* (1932), war in *For Whom the Bell Tolls* (1940), and hunting and fishing in *Green Hills of Africa* (1935) and *The Old Man and the Sea* (1952). Plagued by depression throughout his life, Hemingway shot himself in 1961.

James, Henry (1843–1916): Known later in life as the Master, and with good reason. One of the most important figures in the history of Anglo-American fiction, he produced the first major body of theoretical writing on the novel form. Born in New York City, he spent much of his childhood traveling in Europe. He attended Harvard Law School for a year and was drafted into the army during the American Civil War, but he was exempted from service because of a medical disability. While living in Paris during the mid-1870s, he became acquainted with some of Europe's contemporary novelists; his friends in this period included Ivan Turgenev and Gustave Flaubert. James's early works include *The American* (1877); "Daisy Miller" (1878); and *The Portrait of a Lady* (1882), considered by many his greatest work. He published his most famous story, *The Turn of the Screw*, in 1898. He is said to have experienced a creative rebirth in the early years of the 20th century, producing three astounding novels—*The Wings of the Dove* (1902), *The Ambassadors* (1903), and *The Golden Bowl* (1904)—all celebrated for their close attention to the workings of human consciousness. He lived in England for over 40 years and became a British citizen in 1915. Recently, he has become the subject of other people's fiction, taking the lead role in two interesting novels: Colm Tóibín's *The Master* (2004) and David Lodge's *Author, Author* (2004).

Lahiri, Jhumpa (b. 1967): Short story writer and novelist known for her treatment of the immigrant and postcolonial experience. Born in London, she moved to the United States at the age of three. "I wasn't born here," she once said, "but I might as well have been." Lahiri grew up in Rhode Island and was educated at Barnard College and Boston University, where she received four advanced degrees, including an M.A. in Creative Writing and a Ph.D. in Renaissance Studies. Her first collection of stories, *The Interpreter of Maladies* (1999), enjoyed great success, winning the Pulitzer Prize and the PEN/Hemingway Award. It was also named The New Yorker Debut of the Year. Later publications have included a novel, *The Namesake* (2003), and another collection of stories, *Unaccustomed Earth* (2008). Lahiri has held teaching positions at Boston University and the Rhode Island School of Design. She lives with her family in Brooklyn, New York.

Lewis, C. S. (Clive Staples; 1898–1963): Novelist, critic, and scholar famed for his Christian-themed children's fantasy series *The Chronicles of Narnia*. After his mother died when he was nine, Lewis attended several schools in England and Ireland. He served in the Somerset light infantry division during World War I and was injured in 1918. He received a scholarship to study classics at Oxford after the war. Upon graduating, he began a teaching career at Oxford and Cambridge that spanned nearly four decades. While at Oxford, Lewis was a member of the literary group known as the Inklings, which also included J. R. R. Tolkien and Nevill Coghill. Many of Lewis's works are defenses of his Christian faith, most notably *The Problem of Pain* (1940) and *The Screwtape Letters* (1942)—the latter a satiric work composed of letters from an elderly devil instructing a novice in the art of tempting Christians. His critical works include *The Allegory of Love* (1936) and *An Experiment in Criticism* (1961). Lewis married Joy Gresham in 1956, but she died of cancer in 1960. He wrote movingly of his loss in *A Grief Observed* (1961).

Mansfield, Katherine (1888–1923): Major writer of the modernist period celebrated for her subtle, psychologically sophisticated stories. Born Kathleen Mansfield Beauchamp, she grew up in New Zealand, where her father was a wealthy and influential businessman. She finished her education at Queens College in London and traveled to Paris and Brussels before returning to New Zealand. In 1908, she left New Zealand permanently and moved back to London. After conceiving a child, Mansfield married George Bowden, but she left him after the ceremony. She returned to her previous lover for a month and had a miscarriage shortly thereafter. Hearing of her daughter's licentious behavior and marriage, Mansfield's mother spirited her away to a Bavarian spa. It was here that Mansfield wrote the stories that would compose her first collection, *In a German Pension* (1911). After her brother died in 1915, Mansfield began writing the stories collected in *Prelude* (1918), which focus on family memories in New Zealand. In the last years of her life, she wrote the stories collected in *Bliss* (1920) and *The Garden Party* (1922), which include much of her best work. She died of tuberculosis in 1923.

Munro, Alice (b. 1931): Preeminent Canadian short story writer. Munro was born in southwestern Ontario, where she sets most of her stories. She wrote her first stories as a teenager and first published while studying at Western Ontario University. She left school to get married and move to British Columbia. She and her husband had three children and opened a bookstore. Her first story collection, *Dance of the Happy Shades* (1968), won the Governor General's Award, Canada's highest literary honor, which she has received twice more. In 1972, Munro and her husband divorced, and she moved back to Ontario. She remarried in 1976 and moved to a farm outside Clinton, Ontario. Noteworthy among her 15 published works are *The Love of a Good Woman* (1998) and *Runaway* (2004), both winners of Canada's prestigious Giller Prize. Her stories have frequently been published in *The New Yorker*, *The Atlantic Monthly*, and *The Paris Review*.

O'Connor, Flannery (1925–1964): Catholic novelist and short story writer whose theologically motivated gothic works often blend humorous, violent, and grotesque elements. O'Connor was born in Savannah, Georgia, and attended the Georgia State College for Women, graduating in 1945 with a degree in social science. She attended the Writers' Workshop at the University of Iowa, where she earned an M.F.A. in Creative Writing. Thereafter, she spent three years working on her novel in New York and Connecticut. On a train ride home to the South in 1950, she became seriously ill and was hospitalized in Atlanta. She was diagnosed with lupus, the same disease that had killed her father. After several months of treatment, she moved to a dairy farm with her mother. Her first novel, *Wise Blood*, appeared in 1952, followed by the classic story collection *A Good Man Is Hard to Find*

(1955). O'Connor described the themes of these stories as the workings of grace and original sin. She wrote two more books while her health continued to degenerate. She died of kidney failure in 1964 after her lupus reacted badly to an abdominal surgery.

Poe, Edgar Allan (1809–1849): American short story writer and poet; inventor of the modern detective story and master of macabre fiction. Poe's parents were traveling actors. His father died when he was a year old, leaving his mother to care for him until she died a year later. He was taken into the care of John Allan of Richmond, Virginia. Poe entered the University of Virginia but was forced to leave after amassing large gambling debts. Allan helped him secure a position at West Point, but he was expelled for refusing to participate in drills and classes. By 1831, Poe had published three books of poems, none of which had been commercially successful. As editor of such periodicals as the *Southern Literary Messenger* and *Graham's Magazine*, he published many of his most successful fictions, including "The Fall of the House of Usher" (1839), "The Murders in the Rue Morgue" (1842), and "The Tell-Tale Heart" (1845). He married his 13-year-old cousin Virginia Clemm in 1836. In later years, lack of steady work left the two in desperate financial circumstances. Virginia died of tuberculosis in 1847, two years before Poe died under mysterious circumstances.

Scott, Walter (1771–1832): Scottish poet and novelist credited with the invention of the historical novel. As a young man, Scott apprenticed to become a lawyer, but he preferred to spend his time reading in the six languages he had learned by his midteens. He began his literary career as a translator of Goethe and Bürger, German romantic poets who had a decisive influence on him. His collection of Scottish border ballads, *Minstrelsy of the Scottish Border* (1802–1803), brought him his first taste of literary fame. Shortly thereafter, he began publishing a series of long narrative poems, including *The Lay of the Minstrel* (1805) and *The Lady of the Lake* (1810), his masterpiece of poetic romance. These poems are marked by their Scottish settings, depth of feeling, and striking descriptions of landscape. In 1814, Scott wrote his first novel, *Waverley*, which tells of a young man reaching maturity during the Jacobite uprising in Scotland in 1754–1756. Its popularity prompted Scott to produce a spate of historical novels, including the masterpieces *Rob Roy* (1817) and *Ivanhoe* (1819). He suffered four strokes in his final years, but he continued to write until his death.

 ©2009 The Teaching Company.

Smith, Zadie (b. 1975): Most famous for her images of multiracial, multicultural London, she is also known for her wit, her sensitivity, and her brilliant dialogue. Born to an English father (an advertising executive) and a Jamaican mother (a child psychologist), Smith grew up in the North London neighborhood of Willesden. She attended Cambridge, where she began working on her first novel. Circulated in manuscript, the opening pages set off a bidding war among English publishers. Upon its publication in 2000, *White Teeth* marked Smith as an extravagantly gifted, highly promising writer. She followed her initial success with *The Autograph Man* (2002) and *On Beauty* (2005), a novel informed by her experience as a Radcliffe Fellow at Harvard. Smith borrows much of the structure of *On Beauty* from *Howards End* (1910) and credits E. M. Forster (1879–1970) as a major influence on her work.

Tolstoy, Leo (a.k.a. **Lev Nikolaevich**; 1828–1910): Influential Russian novelist, story writer, and social critic. Tolstoy was born at Yasnaya Polyana to an aristocratic family. His literary career began in the 1850s with the autobiographical trilogy *Childhood* (1852), *Boyhood* (1854), and *Youth* (1857). During the Crimean War, he commanded a battery at the siege of Sebastopol. He married Sonya Andreyevna Behrs in 1862 and had 13 children with her. His first major masterpiece was published between 1865 and 1869: *War and Peace* is an epic story set during Napoleon's invasion of Russia. His other epic masterpiece, *Anna Karenina* (1873–1877), is a romantic novel about adultery and sexual morality. After finishing *Anna Karenina*, Tolstoy underwent a spiritual crisis, resulting in his espousal of a unique, naturalistic brand of Christianity based on the Sermon on the Mount. He devoted the rest of his life to the propagation of this faith. Works such as *The Death of Ivan Ilyich* (1886), *The Kreutzer Sonata* (1891), and the pamphlet *What Is Art* (1898) reflect the intensified moralism of his late period. His family life suffered as a result of his conversion. In his final days, he fled his family in disguise, caught pneumonia, and died of heart failure in a railroad station.

Twain, Mark (1835–1910): Pen name of Samuel Langhorne Clemens, author of *The Adventures of Huckleberry Finn* (1885) and other classic works of American fiction. His father, an attorney, died before Twain reached the age of 11. His formal education has been described as sporadic. His practical education, as a typesetter, riverboat pilot, and reporter, was extensive and transformative. He first used his pseudonym—a term used by pilots to indicate a depth of two fathoms, or about 12 feet—in 1863. (He did not begin to wear his trademark white suit until 1906.) Twain's first literary success came with the publication of "Jim Smiley and His Jumping Frog" in 1865. Highlights of his subsequent career include *Innocents Abroad* (1869), *Roughing It* (1872), *The Adventures of Tom Sawyer* (1876), *A Connecticut Yankee in King Arthur's Court* (1889), and *Pudd'nhead Wilson* (1894). The reputation of *Huck Finn* rests on its complicated (some would say contradictory) treatment of Huck's relationship with Jim, a runaway slave, and on the freshness and vitality of Huck's narration. It is this aspect of the novel that Hemingway seems to have had in mind when he said that "all modern American literature comes from … *Huckleberry Finn*."

Updike, John (1932–2009): Novelist, short story writer, and poet. Updike was born in Reading, Pennsylvania, and grew up in nearby Shillington. He graduated from Harvard University in 1954 and began writing for *The New Yorker* the following year. His first novel, *The Poorhouse Fair* (1958), was a National Book Award finalist. His second novel, *Rabbit, Run* (1960), introduces the character of Harry "Rabbit" Angstrom, a former high school basketball star dissatisfied with his job and marriage. Updike returned to this character in three subsequent novels, *Rabbit Redux* (1971), *Rabbit Is Rich* (1981), and *Rabbit at Rest* (1990). Both of the last two Rabbit novels received Pulitzer Prizes, and the series has become a mainstay of American literature. Updike is the author of over 60 books, including *Pigeon Feathers and Other Stories* (1962), *Couples* (1968), and *In the Beauty of the Lilies* (1996). He described his subject as "the American Protestant small-town middle class." He was also important as a critic of literature and the visual arts. He died of lung cancer in 2009.

Waugh, Evelyn (1903–1966): One of the most respected satirical novelists of the 20th century. Waugh's youth was marked by his intellectual and artistic pursuit. He published an essay on cubism at age 14, founded artistic societies, and won prizes for his art and poetry. He studied at Oxford, where he met Harold Acton. Waugh's first published book, a biography of Dante Gabriel Rossetti, appeared in 1928. It was favorably reviewed but sold poorly. Later that year, Waugh published his first novel, *Decline and Fall*, which brought him fame despite its lack of commercial success. He secured his reputation with novels like *Vile Bodies* (1930) and *A Handful of Dust*

(1934) and became the highest-paid writer of his generation. During World War II, Waugh became an officer in the Royal Marines. He began his most famous novel, *Brideshead Revisited* (1945), while recovering from a minor injury incurred in parachute training. In the mid-1950s, he went mad as a result of bromide poisoning. He recovered and continued writing until his death of a massive coronary thrombosis in 1966.

Wells, H. G. (Herbert George; 1866–1946): English novelist and social commentator known for such classics of science fiction as *The Time Machine* (1895) and *The War of the Worlds* (1898). Wells was the son of shopkeepers. The family lived in dismal conditions and constantly faced the threat of poverty. After a series of failed apprenticeships, he won a scholarship to study biology. He began a career as a science teacher in 1888 and married his cousin shortly thereafter. When the marriage proved unsuccessful, he ran off with a former pupil. Between 1895 and 1908, he published the series of science fiction novels that made him famous. Beginning with *Love and Mr. Lewisham* (1900), he turned increasingly to comic novels about lower-middle-class life, depicting the conditions familiar from his childhood. His earlier writings display an inveterate liberal optimism, but his work grew more bitterly satiric after World War I. In the last decades of his life, Wells concerned himself with popular education and wrote grim, polemical works of fiction.

Wharton, Edith (1862–1937): American novelist and story writer best known for her depictions of upper-class American life. Born to a distinguished New York family, Wharton was educated at private schools in the United States and Europe. She made her society debut in 1879 and married a prominent Boston banker in 1885. She had privately published a book of poems in 1878 but did not start writing seriously until after her marriage. Wharton's first novel, *The Valley of Decision*, appeared in 1902. *The House of Mirth* (1905) was her first critical and popular success. She moved to France in 1907 and divorced her husband in 1913. In France, she deepened her friendship with the novelist Henry James, whose novels had greatly influenced her. This influence is most apparent in *The Age of Innocence* (1920), for which she became the first woman to win the Pulitzer Prize. Other important works include *Ethan Frome* (1911) and *The Custom of the Country* (1915). She continued writing until she suffered a stroke and died at the age of 75.

Woolf, Virginia (1882–1941): Modernist novelist, essayist, and story writer who developed revolutionary narrative techniques in such masterpieces as *Mrs. Dalloway* (1925) and *To the Lighthouse* (1927). Born Adeline Virginia Stephen, Woolf began writing at an early age, composing letters and serial romances with her siblings. Between 1895 and 1904, she endured the loss of her mother, half sister, and father. Strained by her father's death and ongoing sexual abuse by her half brother, Woolf had a nervous breakdown and attempted suicide. After recovering, she moved with her siblings to the Bloomsbury neighborhood of London. Here began the weekly meetings of the radical young artists and intellectuals that came to be known as the Bloomsbury group, which included Clive Bell, Lytton Strachey, John Maynard Keynes, and Woolf's future husband Leonard Woolf, among others. Woolf completed her first novel, *The Voyage Out*, in 1913, but it was not published until 1915 due to another suicide attempt. Subsequent novels such as *Orlando: A Biography* (1928) and *The Waves* (1931) experimented with genre conventions and employed stream-of-consciousness techniques and nonlinear narratives. In her classic feminist work *A Room of One's Own* (1929), Woolf explored the economic and cultural roles of women. In 1941, despairing over the horrors of the war and paralyzed by self-doubt, she loaded her pockets with rocks and walked into the River Ouse.

 ©2009 The Teaching Company.

Bibliography

Abbott, H. Porter. *The Cambridge Introduction to Narrative*. 2nd ed. Cambridge: Cambridge University Press, 2008. Especially helpful on the concept of master plots. Shows how master plots underlie a wide range of narratives, including political campaigns and murder trials.

Amend, Allison. "Dialogue: Talking It Up." In *Writing Fiction: The Practical Guide from New York's Acclaimed Creative Writing School*, by Gotham Writers' Workshop. New York: Bloomsbury, 2003. Argues that "the realism of good dialogue is something of an illusion." Also includes a useful section on subtext.

Amis, Martin. "Waugh's Mag. Op." In *The War against Cliché: Essays and Reviews 1971–2000*. New York: Vintage, 2002. Identifies *Brideshead Revisited* as "lasting schlock," a "really good bad book." A wonderful example of how interpretation and evaluation overlap.

Baxter, Charles. *The Art of Subtext: Beyond Plot*. St. Paul, MN: Graywolf Press, 2007. Essays by a gifted writer and teacher. Tells how stories take us "beyond the plot" and "into the realm of … the implied, the half-visible, and the unspoken."

Bentley, Phyllis. *Some Observations on the Art of Narrative*. New York: Macmillan, 1947. Argues that "the proper use, the right mingling, of scene, description, and summary is the art of fictitious narrative."

Booth, Wayne C. *The Rhetoric of Fiction*. Chicago: University of Chicago, 1962. Groundbreaking work of narrative theory and the source of now-familiar concepts like the implied author and unreliable narrator.

———. *A Rhetoric of Irony*. Chicago: University of Chicago, 1974. Lays out the identifying features of ironic statements, as well as the process by which we reconstruct their intended meanings. Also distinguishes stable irony from unstable irony.

Brooks, Peter. *Reading for the Plot: Design and Intention in Narrative*. New York: Knopf, 1984. Sophisticated discussion of plot, with an emphasis on repetition and reworking. The first chapter includes several pages on Sherlock Holmes.

Burns, Carole, ed. *Off the Page: Writers Talk about Beginnings, Endings, and Everything in Between.* Introduction by Marie Arana. New York: Norton, 2008. Excerpts from interviews originally conducted for washingtonpost.com, with thoughts on many of the issues treated in our course.

Burroway, Janet, and Elizabeth Stuckey-French. *Writing Fiction: A Guide to Narrative Craft.* 7th ed. New York: Longman, 2006. Influential guide for writers. Includes a very helpful chapter on plot and structure, arguing that "*drama* equals *desire* plus *danger*."

Calvino, Italo. "Jorge Luis Borges." In *Why Read the Classics?* New York: Vintage, 2001. A loving tribute, focused largely on Borges's story "The Garden of Forking Paths."

———. "Why Read the Classics?" In *Why Read the Classics?* New York: Vintage, 2001. A playful look at several interlocking questions: What is a classic? Is it ever too late to read the classics? How do you make the classics your own? And more.

Campbell, Joseph. *The Power of Myth.* New York: Anchor Books, 1991. Transcripts of conversations between Campbell and Bill Moyers. Topics include the myth of the hero's adventure or journey.

Carlson, Ron. *Ron Carlson Writes a Story.* St. Paul, MN: Graywolf Press, 2007. The story of a story called "The Governor's Ball," this book takes us from "the first glimmer of an idea to the final sentence." Includes an insightful chapter on writing dialogue.

Cobley, Paul. *Narrative.* New York: Routledge, 2001. Fine introduction to narrative theory. Begins with the distinction between story and plot. Ends with chapters on the emergence of metafiction and the treatment of narrative in cyberspace.

Desmond, John, and Peter Hawkes. *Adaptation: Studying Film and Literature.* New York: McGraw-Hill, 2005. Intelligent and thorough, with chapters on the adaptation of novels, short stories, plays, and works of nonfiction.

Eliot, T. S. "Tradition and the Individual Talent." In *The Norton Anthology of Theory and Criticism*, edited by William E. Cain, Laurie A. Finke, Barbara E. Johnson, John P. McGowan, Jeffrey L. Williams, and Vincent B. Leitch. New York: W. W. Norton, 2001. Enormously influential account of the creative process. Source of the distinction between "the man who suffers" and "the mind which creates."

©2009 The Teaching Company.

Flint, Kate. "The Victorian Novel and Its Readers." In *The Cambridge Companion to the Victorian Novel*, edited by Deirdre David. Cambridge: Cambridge University Press, 2001. Useful for anyone interested in Brontë, Dickens, and Hardy. Helps us to see how their initial readers would have understood and approached their books.

Ford, Richard. "Introduction: Why We Like Chekhov." In *The Essential Tales of Chekhov*. New York: Harper Perennial, 2000. Accounts for Chekhov's influence on later writers. Argues that Chekhov's wish "is to complicate and compromise our view of characters we might mistakenly suppose we could understand with only a glance."

Forster, E. M. *Aspects of the Novel*. Orlando, FL: Harvest Books, 1956. Collects lectures delivered at Cambridge in the spring of 1927. Most famous for its discussion of flat and round characters (in chapter 4) and its definition of "plot" (in chapter 5).

Foster, Thomas C. *How to Read Novels like a Professor: A Jaunty Exploration of the World's Favorite Literary Form*. New York: Harper Paperbacks, 2008. Especially useful for chapter 8, which argues that chapters "achieve small structures in support of the large structure of the book."

Franzen, Jonathan. "Alice's Wonderland." *The New York Times Book Review*, November 14, 2004. Says that Alice Munro has a "strong claim to being the best fiction writer now working in North America." Also lists several reasons why "her excellence so dismayingly exceeds her fame."

————. "Why Bother?" In *How to Be Alone: Essays*. New York: Farrar, Straus and Giroux, 2002. Tough-minded reflections on what reading can and cannot do for us. Also describes Franzen's struggle to find meaning in his own work as a writer.

Frow, John. *Genre*. New York: Routledge, 2005. Argues that genres "actively generate and shape knowledge of the world."

Gornick, Vivian. *The End of the Novel of Love*. Boston: Beacon Press, 1998. Identifies *The Age of Innocence* as one of many classic novels in which love seems to have transforming powers. Are such novels still being written, Gornick asks, and if not, why not?

Hutcheon, Linda. *A Theory of Adaptation*. New York: Routledge, 2006. Asserts that adaptation is "omnipresent in our culture." Concludes that "in the workings of the human imagination, adaptation is the norm, not the exception."

LaPlante, Alice. *The Making of a Story: A Norton Guide to Writing Fiction and Nonfiction*. New York: W. W. Norton, 2007. Splendid advice for beginning writers, with chapters on "why you need to show and tell" and "crafting effective dialogue."

Lewis, C. S. *An Experiment in Criticism*. Cambridge: Cambridge University Press, 1992. A small book full of wonderful observations about reading.

Lodge, David. *The Art of Fiction Illustrated from Classic and Modern Texts*. New York: Penguin, 1994. Delightful collection of newspaper columns, each devoted to an aspect of the writer's craft. Topics include beginning, suspense, introducing a character, and chapters. A classic of its kind.

———. "Mimesis and Diegesis in Modern Fiction." In *After Bakhtin: Essays on Fiction and Criticism*. New York: Routledge, 1990. Influential work of narrative theory. Argues that the relationship between scene (mimesis) and summary (diegesis) changes with the shift from 19th-century realism to 20th-century modernism and postmodernism.

Merkin, Daphne. "Northern Exposures." *The New York Times Magazine*, October 24, 2004. Unusually intelligent profile of short story writer Alice Munro. Praises Munro's fiction for "its clear, unfinicky delineation of complex adult emotions."

Miller, Laura, with Adam Begley, eds. *The salon.com Reader's Guide to Contemporary Authors*. New York: Penguin, 2000. Indispensable guide to 225 contemporary writers. Contributions from leading critics and famous writers. Highlights include John Updike's list of "timeless novels about loving" and Pauline Kael's list of "books that have something to do with movies."

Morson, Gary Saul. "*War and Peace*." In *The Cambridge Companion to Tolstoy*, edited by Donna Tussing Orwin. Cambridge: Cambridge University Press, 2002. Splendid introduction to Tolstoy's novel. Asserts that the novel succeeds not in spite of its loose, baggy structure but because of it.

Muecke, D. C. *Irony*. London: Methuen, 1970. Remains the best introduction to a very slippery topic. Especially good on the distinction between irony and its opposites, earnestness and seriousness.

Mullan, John. *How Novels Work*. New York: Oxford University Press, 2006. Draws on columns originally published in a British newspaper. Treats a wide range of examples with enthusiasm and intelligence.

O'Connor, Flannery. "The Nature and Aim of Fiction." In *Mystery and Manners: Occasional Prose*. New York: Farrar, Straus and Giroux, 1969. Originally given as a talk to students enrolled in a course called How the Writer Writes, this piece asserts that the "least common denominator" of fiction is "the fact that it is concrete."

———. "Writing Short Stories." In *Mystery and Manners: Occasional Prose*. New York: Farrar, Straus and Giroux, 1969. "A story," according to this wonderful essay, "is a way to say something that can't be said any other way."

The Paris Review. *The Paris Review Interviews*. Vols. 1–3. New York: Picador, 2006–2008. Brilliant reflections on the art of fiction writing with authors from Hemingway and Faulkner to Toni Morrison, Alice Munro, and Stephen King.

Prose, Francine. *Reading like a Writer: A Guide for People Who Love Books and for Those Who Want to Write Them*. New York: Harper Perennial, 2007. Urges aspiring writers to master the art of close reading. Devotes its first three chapters to words, sentences, and paragraphs.

Richter, David. *Falling into Theory*. 2nd ed. New York: Bedford/St. Martin's, 1999. Collects "conflicting views on reading literature." Especially useful for essays on interpretation and evaluation. On interpretation, start with Barbara Herrnstein Smith and Harold Bloom. On evaluation, try Stanley Fish, Wayne C. Booth, and Martha Nussbaum.

Robbe-Grillet, Alain. "From Realism to Reality." In *For a New Novel: Essays on Fiction*. Evanston, IL: Northwestern University Press, 1992. Important essay by the writer most closely identified with the *nouveau roman*, or "new novel," of the 1950s. Starts with a bang, announcing that "all writers believe they are realists."

Samet, Elizabeth. *Soldier's Heart: Reading Literature through Peace and War at West Point*. New York: Farrar, Straus and Giroux, 2007. Moving, intelligent reflections on "reading literature through peace and war," written by a member of the English department at West Point. Often stops to consider passages by U. S. Grant, Tim O'Brien, and (of course) Tolstoy.

Scholes, Robert, James Phelan, and Robert Kellogg. *The Nature of Narrative: Revised and Expanded*. Rev. ed. New York: Oxford University Press, 2006. Traces the history of narrative from Homer to Joyce. Places the novel in relation to earlier forms, including epic and folktales.

Shklovsky, Viktor. *Theory of Prose*. Normal, IL: Dalkey Archive Press, 1991. A collection of essays by one of the leading Russian formalists. Includes Shklovsky's discussion of the Sherlock Holmes stories, in which he says that the concept of plot must not be confused with the story line.

Shurtleff, Michael. *Audition: Everything an Actor Needs to Know to Get the Part*. New York: Walker, 2003. Classic text for acting students. Chapter 2 is a virtual master class on "playing the subtext."

Smiley, Jane. *13 Ways of Looking at the Novel*. New York: Anchor, 2006. A writer tries to restore her faith in fiction by reading 100 novels. Impressive chapters on the "psychology of the novel" and the "art of the novel," in addition to brief essays on each of those 100 books.

Tulloch, Graham. "Introduction." In *Ivanhoe*, by Walter Scott. New York: Penguin Classics, 2000. Smart discussion of major themes in Scott's most popular novel.

Updike, John. "*The Age of Innocence*." In *More Matter: Essays and Criticism*. New York: Ballantine Books, 2000. Elegant, economical introduction to Wharton's novel. Places the book in the context of her life and relates it to her reading of Henry James and Marcel Proust.

———. "Why Write?" In *Picked-Up Pieces*. New York: Knopf, 1975. Begins by asking "Why not?" Concludes by describing the writer as "a conduit who so positions himself that the world at his back flows through to the readers on the other side of the page."

Waugh, Patricia. *Metafiction*. New York: Routledge, 1984. Places recent examples in a larger historical context. Also situates those examples on a "sliding scale of metafictional practices."

Whitworth, Michael. *Virginia Woolf*. New York: Oxford University Press, 2009. A fine introduction to Woolf's life and work. Chapter 3 deals with the marketing and consumption of modernist fiction.

Wolf, Maryanne. *Proust and the Squid: The Story and Science of the Reading Brain*. New York: Harper Perennial, 2008. An account of how our brains change as we learn to read.

Wood, James. *How Fiction Works*. New York: Farrar, Straus and Giroux, 2008. A survey of the elements of fiction by a brilliant critic widely regarded as the most perceptive critic of his age. Identifies "the desire to be truthful about life … as a universal literary motive and project."

Credits

Excerpts from "Big Two-Hearted River, Part I" reprinted with the permission of Simon & Schuster, Inc., from THE SHORT STORIES OF ERNEST HEMINGWAY by Ernest Hemingway. Copyright © 1925 by Charles Scribner's Sons. Copyright renewed 1953 by Ernest Hemingway. For UK print rights, excerpts from "Big Two-Hearted River: Part I" from THE FIRST 49 STORIES by Ernest Hemingway, published by Jonathan Cape. Reprinted in the UK by permission of The Random House Group Ltd.

Excerpts from "Pigeon Feathers," from PIGEON FEATHERS AND OTHER STORIES by John Updike, © 1962 and renewed 1990 by John Updike. Used by permission of Alfred A. Knopf, a division of Random House, Inc. For UK print rights: EARLY STORIES by John Updike (Hamish Hamilton, 2004). Copyright © John Updike, 2003. Reproduced in the UK by permission of Penguin Books Ltd.

Excerpts from "Revelation" by Flannery O'Connor © 1956, 1957, 1958, 1960, 1961, 1962, Flannery O'Connor. Copyright renewed 1993 by Regina Cline O'Connor. Reprinted by permission of the Mary Flannery O'Connor Charitable Trust via Harold Matson Company, Inc.

            ©2009 The Teaching Company.

Notes

Notes